Am I On The Sp

An Aspies Guide To The Au

I am On It So Are You!

By Danielle Hampson

ISBN 978-1-9162777-1-7

Book Cover courtesy of Designed Memories Liat Ken-Dror.

Edited By David Hicks

Printed and Bound in England by

Lightening Source UK Ltd. Milton Keynes UK.

Published by Liverbird 2020

www.amionthespectrum.com

With thanks to the people who have inspired me along the way
you know who you are....

For Jamie & Bryana

Be somebody who makes everyone
feel like a somebody

Always follow your dreams

Mum x

"A Spectrum is used to classify something in terms of its position on a scale between two extreme points"

Table of Contents

Chapter 1

Am I On The Spectrum?

An Aspies Guide to The Autistic Spectrum

I am on it and so are you!.

After the birth of our first child and the health problems we encountered with our son, like many new mothers anxiety sets in, but with the birth it led me onto the path of self discovery. My son's condition at that time had no name, let alone a diagnosis, and was to several medical professionals a complete and utter mystery. By the time my son reached the age of 6, after several years of unsuccessful diagnosis, the words Asperger's Syndrome were first mentioned to me by a doctor at Alder Hay Hospital in Liverpool Merseyside. Trying to absorb this new information in a state of shock, it took me 3 months before I picked up my first book on the subject of Autism. Together with having a second child with the same condition two years younger, followed by a divorce, I started to formulate my own theories on how I ended up here and how Autism impacts everyone's life not only my own.

An Aspies guide to the Autistic Spectrum – I am on it so are you! Was largely born out of my own experience with people in my everyday life as everyone was looking for answers as to what the Spectrum consisted of? I initially started out in my first career as a Beauty Therapist in my late teens early 20's, following on for a 25 year career as TV Producer/Entertainment Film and TV Publicist and now due to my life experiences in the latter part of my life, where I retrained as a Counsellor Psychotherapist. Today in my late 40's I work with a range of personality problems, addictions, victims of domestic violence, perpetrators of violence, sex offenders and substance misusers on a daily basis. As my client base grows both in professional private practice and in the voluntary charity sector, all of my clients past and present together with the range of people friends and business clients I have had the pleasure of knowing have enriched my life for better or worse.

I believe everyone has a range of Autism Spectrum features that may or may not have not yet been clinically identified and academically validated, which should form part of the Autism Spectrum. They are defined in the DSM Fifth Edition Journal (Diagnostic and Statistical Manual of Mental Health Conditions) but have not yet been attributed to what is the Autism Spectrum and the Autism Spectrum is huge.

This book is based on my theories as a trained psychotherapist. I would like to stress I am not a qualified doctor nor am I trained medical professional. My experience is largely based on the clients that I see in a clinical setting and the problems and complexities they have in their everyday lives with social communication, understanding and self awareness of the impact of their actions on others. Some of my theories have been academically validated, some await academic validation, but as I write this book whispers in PhD documents, journals and articles are starting to influence into mainstream clinical settings, but largely this book is based around my experience of the human personality traits that signify coincidental patterns of behaviour and medical conditions, that have many similarities with Autistic patterns and traits, that I have witnessed in the clinical setting of the counselling room as well as, with my life experience of meeting people and personalities. I am not here to confuse you the reader by particular traits of behaviour compared to a being in possession of a full diagnostic assessment. Nor am I pathologising numbers of people or about encouraging diagnostic inflation. We will not be looking in any depth at the more severe learning difficulties of more extreme types of autism.

This book will question and hopefully raise assumptions about our mental health, what is 'typical' or 'normal' which could be empowering to individuals reading when reading this book you must be mindful of the fact that a Spectrum is used to classify something in terms of its position on a scale between two extreme points. This book will challenge the current theories suggesting you are either are a neuro typical NT (ie: you don't have Autism or Asperger's Syndrome or you do?) not displaying or characterised by Autistic or other neurologically atypical patterns of thought or behaviour. What we currently believe is the ASD Spectrum extends over a wide range of traits and behaviours in terms of variety, intensity, personal impact and the impact it has on others. What I believe is that this book is offering permission to everyone wishing to seek an assessment in early, middle or late adulthood to find out if you actually are on the Spectrum, this book is also designed for people to recognise traits of behaviour in themselves or others, that may have an association with the ASD Spectrum and this book is designed for those who are seeking to offer compassionate help in dealing with such traits or behaviour in themselves and others; and the text of this book offers cautious recognition to the idea that persons on the ASD Spectrum who associate these behaviours should celebrate their strengths and acknowledge their weaknesses.

What we seem to have determined along is that these behaviour patterns and Autistic traits are in every one of us, however there is a 25 year gap of waiting for scientific research to filter down into mainstream clinical medical practices, many individuals are left isolated struggling and waiting for answers as to why they are the way they are and what can be done about it. Children have increasingly been being diagnosed with Asperger's Syndrome and their behaviour is explained as Autistic from mid 2000 and beyond; many parents have been left feeling vulnerable, baffled and confused as to why their children have this diagnosis and what can be done about it. This influx of over whelming words has inundated health professionals NHS resources, and Autism organisations where some people have begun a personal quest feeling the need for coping strategies and solutions to the many unanswered questions about how to just get through the day.

Here in the UK more and more resources are becoming available, but what about generations of parents, grandparents or great grandparents that have been largely left behind from the 1940's up to the present day many have never been assessed or had the chance to even understand if their own behaviours are on the Autism Spectrum. There are six generations of people who have little knowledge or education about what Asperger's or Autism actually is, let alone whether they have contributed to it genetically how they might obtain a diagnosis themselves. Today there is no definition of what the Autism Spectrum looks like let alone what it consists of, but I hope writing this book will help educate people further into what practice is slow to achieve.

Currently nearly all Autism related books refer to the condition and the persons who have it as AS (Autism Spectrum) individuals, they draw a comparison with individuals who do not have the condition known as NT's (Neurotypicals) or non AS (Autism Spectrum) individuals. But what would happen if we turn current science and all knowledge that exists about the condition on its head and suggest that there is no NT's. What if everyone we meet on a daily basis has some features of Autism and Asperger's Syndrome but we just don't actually realise it yet? What if science hasn't caught up with the different personality types, and nearly everyone that you meet exists in one form or other on the Autism Spectrum, with some behaviours are leaning towards one specific personality type or a cluster of other types of sub behaviours.

Many people are frustrated in their relationship's, many people displaying Autism and Asperger's character traits mildly or in greater forms. Many people are in relationships with and love people with these character traits, but when there is tension they do not know what to do to make things better? Many people make things worse by 'killing' their loved ones with kindness or by enabling their loved one's behaviour, where there is tension, as they have no real clue as they do not know what to do to make things better. Through understanding how highly varied men and women are on the Autism Spectrum we can learn new ways to successfully relate with, listen to and support our loved ones by understanding their behaviour better. This is what this book is designed to do.

But what if your eyes were opened a lot more fully to lots of different personality types that you hadn't even considered before, that could possibly be on the Autism Spectrum? Would it make a difference as to how you see and deal with people on a day to day basis? Would it open your eyes to being a more compassionate person to their personality type? Would it give you greater understanding how to deal with those individuals? Or would it still end in frustration? Men are from Aspie Land Woman are Too will look at the different personality types of individuals and draw comparisons of behaviour to the way people are that you've never thought about before, looking at the different personality types that have not yet been linked to Autism Spectrum.

The words Autism is everywhere often without formal explanation. Channel 4 ran an Autism Season followed by the BBC running a successful TV series called the A word where the key protagonist character was a small boy named Joe. The BBC series highlighted family tensions that arose from living with the condition.

The condition is everywhere, the words are everywhere. CH4's Udateables looks at dating with what can best be described in most cases as high functioning Autistic individuals and how daters relate to each other reflect other TV programmes have covered ADHD awareness, or Me and My Tourette's and ITV School for Stammers. Whilst there are all mainly positive outcomes these raise the awareness of conditions that were once a taboo. Some people view these conditions as learning disabilities that can hold people back in society, other people view them as a nervous or involuntary condition. With wider education instead of turning people into everyday freaks shows, by goggle boxing and highlighting their issues into mini forms of stardom, fandoms of reality TV, what would you the reader think if I were to say that all these learning disabilities plus many more are actually part of the Autism Spectrum?

TV programmes highlight celebrities and athletes who in later life have discovered that their quirkiness and ability have been a contributing factor to the role that they have learnt to live with, some of which is attributed positively and some of it has attributed negatively. Some people attribute their character to a mental health condition that needs to be kept in check. I notice that at least three times a week I am told (or I tell someone) that I think they should consider they may be on the Spectrum and what their personality traits are indicating and maybe for homework they should do some research in this area as it may help them to come to a conclusion as to why they behave in a certain way. Could this mean that we could be on the cusp of a diagnostic inflation or are we already in one?

The diagnosis is used everywhere: Facebook's former head of engineering has stated that Mark Zuckerberg has "a touch of the Asperger's." Time Magazine suggested that the intensely awkward Bill Gates is Autistic. Is much of this a requisite of popular psychology and speculation do they have traits associated with the condition or do they actually have the condition? Most people will remember at school the wild naughty boy that was always in trouble that was in their class, or the boy that had ants in his pants that wouldn't sit still, the boy or girl that was terribly brainy, a little professor, or the child that was geeky that probably didn't have many friends. Then there was always the sporty one that always won all the cups medals and trophies, that excelled at every sport not just one. There was the shy child that was slow to speak, the one that bullies always picked on and didn't stand up for himself, the one that was never the cool kid with dorky glasses, a bad haircut and uncool trainers! Or the child that had amazing natural artistic abilities or the mathematics or language genius... But what if we now know these characteristics or traits might be attributed to Autism would we have viewed things differently as children? The current school of thought is that you as Autistics persons we tend to excel in one or more of these 7 key areas: regardless of intelligence. Mathematics, Science, Languages, Music, Art, or Sport, or Business.

Still others are seeing it in themselves. David Byrne: "I was a peculiar young man - borderline Asperger's, I would guess. Craig's list founder

Craig Newmark, noting his poor eye contact and limited social competency, blogged that Asperger's symptoms "feels uncomfortably familiar." Dan Aykroyd confessed that he was diagnosed with Asperger's as a child (a puzzling claim given that the diagnosis didn't exist prior to 1981, when Aykroyd turned 29) Aykroyd insisted he was being serious, and as evidence of his continuing symptoms he noted his "fascination with law enforcement and the police."

What is happening? What cultural look like has emerged that would join such surreal life bedfellows as a pop piano playing crooner, a flamboyant professional basketball player, a reclusive children's book author, a twenty something Internet gazillionaire, and a genocidal madman together in diagnostic brotherhood? How have we reached a point where these partisans of left and right can regard the opposing candidates for the highest office in the land and see... an arcane brain disorder? "It's an epidemic, Or else a wildly over diagnosed thing that there used to be other words for it. Or perhaps there were no real words to describe it all and we just took it as normal, until normal no longer became a word to sub categorise and label certain people as being significantly different.

Every generation has its defining psychiatric malady, confidently diagnosed from afar by armchair non psychiatrists. In the fifties, all those grey suited organisation men were married to "frigid" women. Until a few years ago, the country of self obsessed boomers, reality TV fame seekers and vain politicians and bubble riding Ponzi schemers made "narcissistic personality" disorder a diagnosis in the American Psychiatric Association's Diagnostic and Statistical Manual of Mental Disorders, fourth edition the craziness of the moment. And who among us has not proudly copped to our own "OCD" or "ADD," where we have deemed a mercurial sibling "seriously bipolar," written off an erratic ex as "obviously borderline," or nodded enthusiastically as a newly redundant friend pronounced his former boss a "textbook sociopath"?

Lately, a new kind of head case stalks the land staring past us, blurting gaucheries, droning on about the technical minutiae of his boring hobby. And we are ready with our DSM Diagnostic Statistical Manual Codes: 299.00 (Autistic disorder) and 299.80 (Asperger's disorder). The pros have led the way. In the nineties, clinicians began reconceptualising Autism from a singular disorder to a cluster of related conditions on a spectrum of severity, as the criteria broadened to encompass less acutely impaired people such as the more verbal group diagnosed with Asperger's prevalence rose dramatically. Before 1980, one in 2,000 children was thought to be autistic. By 2007, the Centres for Disease Control were reporting that one in 152 American children had an Autism Spectrum Disorder. Two years later, the CDC updated the ratio to one in 110. By March 2012, the CDC revised the number upward again, to one in 88 (one in 54, if you just count boys, who are five times as likely to have the condition than girls). A South Korean study from the same year put the number even higher, at one in 38. And in New Jersey, according to the numbers, an improbable one in 29 boys is on the spectrum. 2018 Barron-Cohn research suggests it may be a male to female ratio of 3:1 and yet the Cambridge researcher only attributes it to 1% of the population that is without taking the other personality types into account. His studies are purely on the basis of the diagnostic criteria, that exists for specific character traits in childhood but not all of them and furthermore now suggests that Autism and Asperger's Syndrome are hereditary genetically linked.

Despite much debate about the causes of the so called Autism epidemic, the consensus among experts is that the increase is mostly due not to a rise in incidence but to greater awareness, recognition, and testing, and to the wider parameters of who qualifies for a place on the Spectrum. Such elasticity is nowhere so relevant as at the fuzzy, ever shifting threshold where clinical disorder shades into everyday eccentricity. The upper end of the spectrum is the liminal zone where Aspies, as people with Asperger's call themselves, reside.

But this story about Asperger's, Autism, or the Spectrum or those very real afflictions that can bring untold hardship to the people who suffer from them and to their families. This book is, instead, a story about

"Asperger's," "Autism," and "The Spectrum" our one stop shopping shorthand for the jerky husband, the socially inept plutocrat, the tactless boss, the child prodigy with no friends, the remorseless criminal. It's about the words we deploy to describe some murky hybrid of egghead and the aloof.

Like the actual clinical disorder, the cultural epidemic in scare quotes may have less to do with changes in the world than with changes in those seeing it. To some degree, The Spectrum is our way of making sense of an upended social topography, a buckled landscape where nerd titans hold the high ground once occupied by square jawed captains of industry, a befuddling digital world overrun with trolls and avatars and social media rock stars who are nothing like actual rock stars but employ a character trait known as narcissism. It is, as the amateur psychologists would have it, a handy phrase for the distant, cerebral men with the ambition and self possession necessary to mount a serious run for Prime Minister. As the coders inherit the Earth, saying someone's on The Spectrum is how English majors make themselves feel better.

But when anxiety alone doesn't fully explain it? Does the bi polar depressive swing do it instead? Or perhaps it's the Paranoid Schitzoid position of having a split personality that can be attributed to the star sign of a Gemini. There's something admiring, too, in the cultural uses of Asperger's Syndrome, which makes it different from the psych put downs du jour of previous eras. The popular but mostly over used image of Dustin Hoffman's Rain Man make asocial geniuses or whether the sitcom Big Bang Theory and Community, has helped create a mystique around high functioning Autism, and the idea that Asperger's offers selective advantages has midwifed a generation of self-outers. For example, Pulitzer Prize winning music critic Tim Page's Parallel Play: Growing Up With Undiagnosed Asperger's, and contestant Heather Kuzmich's appearances on America's Next Top Model, or singer songwriter Toyah Wilcox dyslexia are all great visual examples. So we find ourselves in a weird place it soothes the insecurities of those who would weaponise it as an insult, it flatters the vanity of those who'd appropriate it as status credential.

Yet the yen to see the world in Spectrum Vision is not just a case of glib metaphor abuse. Some studies of twins suggest that Autism traits are distributed throughout the population. And it's now understood that there's an Autism phenotype, (a set of observable characteristics that are due to the environment or exacerbated in some environments) where the same genetics can manifest in mild forms in parents and grandparents as full blown Autism in their children and grandchildren.

No one has been so responsible for the spread of this idea as Baron-Cohen, who has conducted a number of studies showing concentrations of Autism among techies of the computer world. In 1997, he published one asserting that Autistic children were twice as likely as non Autistic children to have fathers or grandfathers who were engineers. He found a higher rate of Autistic traits among math students at Cambridge than among those in other disciplines, and he has argued that in Silicon Valley, geeks intermarry and are more likely to produce Autistic offspring. So does that mean my theory could be nearer a conclusion that every one is on the Spectrum somewhere, not just the ones that marry and produce offspring like for like?

As it turns out, a striking number of criminal defendants diagnosed with Asperger's are computer hackers. Carrying this theory over many people marry or form partnerships with their Autistic opposite. Computer hackers are often people on The Spectrum who end up outside the law by default their lack of social skills combined with a surplus of computer know how. The Internet is what has made them it has given them a place to be criminals.

The self diagnosis boom has been accompanied by self diagnoses that can be bracing in their un persuasiveness. Aspies who self diagnose and otherwise, speak of the relief that a diagnosis brings to them. For someone who may have gone decades feeling socially alienated, and blaming themselves for it; knowledge of the condition can offer a key to the puzzle of their personality and the interpersonal challenges they have experienced. It was "a biblical weight off," and an explanation for all those social banana peels along the way. Stuart Duncan, is the author of the "Autism Blog" called "Autism From a Father's Point of View" and also the founder of "Autcraft", the first Minecraft server for children with Autism and their families. He was diagnosed with Asperger's as an adult after his son was diagnosed with PDD-NOS at the age of 2. (PDD-NOS stands for Pervasive Developmental Disorder-Not Otherwise Specified).

Less grandly, there may be something to the idea of an affinity between Autistics and the Information Age, given that Autistics, with their difficulty imagining minds apart from their own, tend to relate better to animals and machines than to people. Online, the off putting physical manifestations of Spectrum disorders are stripped away. Celebrity Autistic Temple Grandin has said that "there is nothing out there closer to how I think" than the web, with its structure of associative links. The web is shaping our behaviour in "what is broadly a more autistic direction.

If you were to get rid of all the Autism genetics, there would be no more Silicon Valley," Grandin told an audience. David Mamet, in his book Bambi vs. Godzilla, writes, "I think it is not impossible that Asperger's syndrome helped make the movies," citing such movie director traits as "early precocity," high information processing capacity, visuality, creativity, attachment to routine, unconventionality, and social deficits. A recent ripple of business journalism has emphasized the narrow competencies of those on the high-functioning end of The Spectrum as a competitive advantage so If you really want to innovate, put an Autistic Person on your team. Specialist erne, a Danish company, employs 60 people on The Spectrum to do software testing and other repetitive tasks. Some Autistics' "cognitive strengths" are better at noticing details in patterns, they have better eyesight on average, they are less likely to be fooled by optical illusions... and they are less likely to have false memories of particular kinds.

However the number of registered users of the original PC version of Minecraft reached 100's of millions, creator Markus Persson announced via Twitter. The game is also available on Xbox, which has sold over 10 million copies, on PlayStation, over 1 million copies, and a 'pocket edition' which is available for phones and tablets, that has sold over 10 million copies. The word Minecraft is Googled more than the Bible, Justin Bieber and Harry Potter. But Markus Persson's remarkable journey from shy computer geek to billionaire entrepreneur as one of the lead co creators of the successful children's game Minecraft is all the more incredible given the tragedy he has overcome. His father Birger Persson, who had battled with drug abuse since before his son was born, shot himself in the head just before Christmas in 2011, while in the depth of depression. Markus younger sister Anna, whose smiling face and tattooed body hide her own years of addiction, ran away from home as teenager and also turned to drugs. His hard working mother, Ritve, a Finnish born nurse who supported him through his troubled adolescence, and encouraged his interest in computers, also had problems when she was young. At some point, the demons that haunted Markus' father returned too and he fell back into the spiral of drink and drugs. Is there a strong link between substance misuse and the Autistic brain? Perssons is but just one well known case example as Am I On The Spectrum? An Aspies Guide To The Autistic Spectrum - I am on it and so are you? will explore substance misuse and its impact on how the Autistic brain works.

The same rose coloured impulse has driven an Aspie wave of revisionists in which such diverse historical figures as Thomas Jefferson, Orson Welles, Charles Darwin, Albert Einstein, Isaac Newton, Andy Warhol, and Wolfgang Amadeus Mozart are supposed to all have been residents of the Spectrum. This is a positive outlook of how Asperger Talents Changed the World.

For clinicians in the trenches, the more exuberant efforts to link Autism with genius can be exasperating. Do blind people hear music more exquisitely than people with sight? We don't have any neuro physiological evidence that they do. Similarly, most people with Asperger's have average intelligence, with high IQs the exception but not necessarily so in the case of many with Dyslexia. Do people who have one sense impaired out of the five feel much strong senses across the other four, for example a blind person may have much stronger acute hearing, or a very vivid sense of smell or taste. Do some Aspies have a stronger sense in one sensory area than in others? For example are their senses on high alert with eyes smell and taste. Do people on the Autism Spectrum lose their sense of hearing earlier than others?

The prevalence of Autistic Spectrum Disorders (ASD) is higher in deaf people than in hearing people. However, conditions that mimic ASD associated with language deprivation are even higher. Additionally, some people who have ASD appear to have an uncomfortable relationship with sound. What we do know is that deaf people can struggle with syntax which can limit understanding and ability to respond appropriately. Many people on the Spectrum diagnosed or not can struggle with hearing, zoning sounds in and out of which they do not have control which seems to also attribute to limiting them processing the ability of information.

The causes of ASD are still not really understood. Whilst a genetic link has been confirmed, there are also causal associations between neurological vulnerability and ASD. As survival rates for infants with these problems rise, there is 20% predicted increase in deafness in the following 20 years.

For a lot of the people, Autism and Asperger's isn't their only problem. "Autism, Bipolar, Borderline Personality Disorder, Depression, Anxiety, Anorexia Eating Disorders, Learning Disabilities, Domestic Abuse, Addictions, Gender related issues, Behavioural and Personality Disorders. Autism Spectrum Disorder (ASD) involves widespread difficulties in social interaction, communication, and behavioural flexibility. Consequently, individuals with ASD are believed to exhibit a number of unique personality tendencies, including a lack of insight into them.

For people Asperger's, Autism or Autism Spectrum Disorder (ASD) is an identity as much as a diagnosis, and it is important to remember that men and women have different personalities and natures, Men and women need to appreciate these differences and cease expecting each other to act and feel the way they do. We hope you will not think that this book is ethnocentric, we have taken steps to provide as much due diligence as is possible. Much of this is a specialist debate with real world implications (insurance, school services, having what is classed as a mental health disorder). We would say, if the term Asperger's Syndrome helps you describe yourself and gives you community, use it! Equally by being ethnographic, if it helps you to learn about particular behaviours and to know how to address those often associated with Autism, where we will explore many of these in the forthcoming chapters.

Chapter 2

Why Does It Happen And Can We Fix It?

As defined by the National Autistic Society (2016) Autism is a lifelong developmental disability that affects how people perceive the world and interact with others. Autistic people see, hear and feel the world differently to other people. If you are Autistic, you are Autistic for life; Autism is not an illness or disease and cannot be 'cured'. Often people feel being Autistic is a fundamental aspect of their identity.

Autism is a spectrum condition which means there are many shades of grey in between, not just black and white behaviour. All Autistic people share certain difficulties, or attributes depending on how you see it, but being Autistic will affect them in different ways. Some Autistic people also have learning disabilities, mental health issues or other conditions, meaning people need different levels of support. All people on the Autism Spectrum learn and develop, with the right sort of support; all can be helped to live a more fulfilling life of their own choosing.

Autism is much more common than most people think. People from all nationalities and cultural, religious and social backgrounds can be Autistic. Although it appears to affect more men than women, that is because many women have softer Autistic traits and can sometimes go under the radar of detection. They may cope better than their Autistic male counterparts, or that they may be very competent at mirroring other peoples behaviour.

Some Autistic people say the world feels overwhelming which can cause them considerable anxiety. In particular, understanding and relating to other people, and taking part in everyday family, school, work and social life, can be harder. Other people appear to know, intuitively, how to communicate and interact with each other, yet can also struggle to build rapport with Autistic people. Autistic people may wonder why they are 'different' and feel their social differences mean people don't understand them.

Autistic people often do not 'look' disabled. Some parents of Autistic children say that other people simply think their child is naughty, while adults find that they are misunderstood. A diagnosis is the formal identification of Autism, usually by a multi disciplinary diagnostic team, often including a speech and language therapist, paediatrician, psychiatrist and/or psychologist or educational psychologist. A diagnosis benefits by providing a timely and thorough assessment and formulation, and may be helpful because it helps Autistic people (and their families, partners, employers, colleagues, teachers and friends) to understand why they may experience certain difficulties and what they can do about them. It thus allows people to access services and support more readily, and some previously had an ADHD diagnosis.

But how is Autism is diagnosed? The characteristics of Autism vary from one person to another. In order for a diagnosis to be made, a person will usually be identified as having had persistent difficulties with social communication and social interaction and restricted and repetitive patterns of behaviours, activities or interests since early childhood, to the extent that these "limit and impair everyday functioning".

People can be puzzled by the diagnosis they or their child have been given. Over the years, different terms have been used for Autism. This reflects the different Autism profiles presented by individuals, and the diagnostic manuals and tools used. Misdiagnosis adds to the range of terms people hear. Autism is a Spectrum condition which means there are many varied parts to it. All Autistic people share certain difficulties, but being Autistic will affect them in different ways. These differences, along with differences in diagnostic approach, have resulted in a variety of terms being used to diagnose Autistic people. Terms that have been used include Autism, Autism Spectrum disorder (ASD), Autism Spectrum Condition (ASC), Atypical Autism, Classic Autism, Kanner Autism, Savant Autism, Pervasive Developmental Disorder (PDD), High-functioning Autism (HFA), Asperger Syndrome and Pathological Demand Avoidance (PDA).

Because of recent and upcoming changes to the main diagnostic manuals, 'Autism Spectrum Disorder' (ASD) is now likely to become the most commonly given diagnostic term. However, clinicians will still often use additional terms to help to describe the particular Autism profile presented by an individual. Some Autistic people also have learning disabilities, mental health issues or other combined conditions. (In this book I will explain the different titles as I see them).

Aspergers Syndrome

A clinician might describe someone as having an Asperger Syndrome profile if there has been no clinically significant delay in language or cognitive development but they still have social communication difficulties. They may also have specific delays in motor development as well as motor 'clumsiness'. People with Asperger Syndrome are of average or above average intelligence. They don't have the severe learning disabilities that many Autistic people have, but they may have specific learning difficulties. They have fewer problems with speech but may still have difficulties with understanding and processing language. For example, they may have a learning impairment such as dyscalculia, dyslexia, dysgraphia and dyspraxia. Some people with Asperger Syndrome say the world feels overwhelming and this can cause them considerable anxiety. In particular, understanding and relating to other people, and taking part in everyday family, school, work and social life, can be harder, exhausting and overwhelming. Other people appear to know, intuitively, how to communicate and interact with each other, yet they can also struggle to build rapport with people with Asperger Syndrome and feel their social differences mean people don't understand them.

For clarification if we view the word "Autism" as meaning more severe an impairment and the word "Aspergers" as having milder traits this will help in our understanding. Where people on the Spectrum, including those with Asperger Syndrome, often do not 'look' disabled, they have cognitive disabilities as opposed to physical difficulties with interpreting both verbal and non-verbal language which can include gestures, facial expressions, understand jokes or humour or tone of voice, understanding empathy or social or moral reasoning. Many have a very literal understanding of language, and think people always mean exactly what they say. They may find it difficult to understand or have an over awareness of facial expressions, tone of voice, jokes and sarcasm, vagueness and abstract concepts.

People with Asperger Syndrome usually have good language skills, where languages including English and journalism could be a special interest; or they could have no interest or ability in languages at all. But they may still find it hard to understand the expectations of others within conversations, perhaps repeating what the other person has just said (this is called echolalia) or talking at length about their own interests, unaware of their surroundings or the fact that they may have talked the listener into submission. It often helps people with Asperger's Syndrome if we speak in a clear, consistent way and give people time to process what has been said to them as some people on the Spectrum process information at slower speeds than other people, this may be due to the fact that they are taking in so much other information from their surrounding environment such as back ground noise, light, smells etc.

People with Asperger Syndrome can often have difficulty 'reading' other people - recognising or understanding others' feelings and intentions - and expressing their own emotions. Or they over empathise with people's feelings and emotions these people are known as 'empaths'. This can make it very hard for them to navigate the social world. They may appear to be insensitive or overly empathetic, seek out time alone when overloaded by other people, not seek comfort from other people, appear to behave 'strangely' or in a way thought to be socially inappropriate.

People on the Spectrum may find it hard to form friendships. Some may want to interact with other people and make friends, but may be unsure how to go about it. Or some people may be so overly empathetic to others needs they can become exploited and used by someone who takes their vulnerability as weakness, empaths believe that they are being empathetic to a situation, place, person they keep repeating the behaviour in the hope to gain the recognition they so badly crave. People on the Spectrum very seldom learn from mistakes and usually keep repeating the same behaviour which is the downside to their vulnerability.

The world can seem a very unpredictable and confusing place to people with Asperger Syndrome, who often prefer to have a daily routine so that they know what is going to happen every day. They may want to always travel the same way to and from school or work, or eat exactly the same food for breakfast, lunch or dinner. Anything deviating from this routine can cause some one a problem. The use of rules can also be important. It may be difficult for someone to take a different approach to something once they have been taught the 'right' way to do it. They may not be comfortable with the idea of change, but may be able to cope better if they can prepare for changes in advance.

Many people with Asperger Syndrome have intense and highly focused interests, often from a fairly young age. These can change over time or become life long passions, and can be anything from art or music, to trains or computers. An interest may sometimes be unusual. One person loved collecting rubbish, for example, with encouragement, the person developed an interest in recycling and the environment. Many channel their interest into studying, paid work, volunteering, or other meaningful occupations. People with Asperger Syndrome often report that the pursuit of such interests is fundamental to their well-being and happiness.

People with Asperger Syndrome may also experience over or under sensitivity to sounds, touch, tastes, smells, light, colours, temperatures or pain. For example, they may find certain background sounds, which other people ignore or block out, unbearably loud or distracting. This can cause anxiety or even physical pain such as migraines. Or they may be fascinated by lights or spinning objects.

Pathological Demand Avoidance

A clinician might describe a person as having a demand avoidant profile, or Pathological Demand Avoidance (PDA), if they are driven to excessively avoid demands and expectations. Underpinning this avoidance is an extremely high level of anxiety about conforming to social demands and of not being in control of the situation. People with a demand avoidant profile can appear to have better social understanding and communication skills than others on the Autism Spectrum, and are often able to use this to their advantage and can often appear manipulative. However, they might not really have as good an understanding of social matters as it seems, they lack substance and mask or copy behaviours and are superficially able but lacking in depth.

PDA affects people from all backgrounds and nationalities. The cause of this, along with other Autism profiles, is still being investigated. Demand Avoidant Behaviour Profiles are seen in people of all genders, and this seems to be in equal proportions. This means that women are as likely to have this profile as men. There are no prevalence figures as yet, but these will become more apparent as more people with a PDA profile are identified. There is increasing recognition of PDA as an Autism behaviour profile.

PDA has also been described as being so overly sensitive to the demands of others, that it creates the need to avoid, which is why when dealing with a PDA personality, the use of language and how you phrase sentences is highly important for otherwise the demands will cause the PDA person to be in information overload, cause anxiety and in order to calm down the PDA person may have a melt down which could include crying, temper tantrum or a physical outburst of aggressive behaviour.

The distinctive features of a Demand Avoidant Profile include resisting and avoiding the ordinary demands of life, using social strategies as part of avoidance, eg: distracting, giving excuses, appearing sociable, but lacking understanding. There may experiences excessive mood swings and impulsivity, they may appear comfortable in role play and pretence. Obsessive behaviour may be often focused on other people. People with this profile can appear controlling and dominating, especially when they feel anxious. However, they can also be enigmatic and charming when they feel secure and in control. It's important to acknowledge that these people have a hidden disability.

People with a Demand Avoidant Profile are likely to need a lot of support. The earlier the recognition of PDA, the sooner appropriate support can be put in place. According to the Elizabeth Newson Centre, many people with a PDA behaviour profile have had a passive early history. As an infant grows, and more is expected of them, they can begin to strongly object to and resist normal demands. A few actively resist from the start as everything is on their own terms and they often display passive aggressive behaviours.

Many parents of children with a Demand Avoidant Profile feel that they have been wrongly accused of poor parenting through a lack of understanding. These parents need a lot of support, as their children can present with severe behavioural challenges. The main characteristic of PDA is a high level of anxiety when demands are placed on that person. Demand avoidance can be seen in the development of children, including those on the Autism Spectrum. It's the extent and extreme nature of this avoidance, together with displays of socially shocking behaviour that leads to it being described as 'pathological'. People with PDA can appear to be very stressed by even simple everyday expectations and they may attempt to avoid these to a remarkable extent. Demands might include a suggestion that it's time to get up, go out of the house or join an activity. At times any suggestion made by another person can be perceived as a demand. This may even be the case when the person seems to want to do what has been suggested.

For some, avoidance may seem their greatest social and cognitive skill and the strategies they use are essentially socially strategic. These can include: distracting the person making the demand, acknowledging the demand but excusing themselves, procrastination and negotiation, physically incapacitating themselves, withdrawing into fantasy, physical outbursts or attacks. Underpinning this avoidance is an anxiety about conforming to social demands and of not being in complete control of the situation. This often becomes very exhausting for the person on the receiving end of the demand avoidant person and can often be perceived as the difficulties being experienced by both parties are way beyond any normal comprehension.

People with other Autism profiles may also react to social demands by becoming avoidant but tend to do this in ways that aren't very social in nature by ignoring, withdrawing or walking away. Someone with a Demand Avoidant Profile may seem to have enough social understanding to adapt their strategies to the person making the demand others may not. Parents very often use the term 'manipulative' to describe this aspect of their child's behaviour and will comment on how it seems to be their greatest skill, often saying "if only they would put half the effort in to doing what it was I wanted as they do to getting out of it."

Those with PDA may also use straightforward refusal or outbursts of explosive behaviour, including aggression. This is probably a form of panic on their part and is usually displayed when other strategies haven't worked or when their anxiety is so high that they 'explode' or have a 'meltdown'. This can be suddenly shouting, screaming, throwing things and physically lashing out.

People with a PDA tend to appear social at first and be 'people-orientated', have learnt many social niceties, may decline a request or suggestion politely, they may seem well tuned in to what might prove effective as a strategy with a particular person, or be unsubtle and lack depth. They can be misleading, overpowering or may overreact to seemingly trivial events, They can have difficulty seeing boundaries, accepting social obligation and taking responsibility for their actions, displaying confusing behaviour and contradictory moods. Hugging becomes pinching or a child may embrace their parent while saying something like "I hate you", or be disconnected from their feelings, feeling nothing, or they may say they don't feel something when indeed they do. As children or adults, they may of lack a sense of pride or embarrassment, and behave in uninhibited ways, failing to understand the unwritten social boundaries that exist between adults and children and can become overfamiliar or bossy. They may treat everyone the same with no sense of authority and don't recognise a hierarchy.

People with PDA experience difficulty with regulating emotions, which is common more generally in Autistic people, but early studies found it especially prevalent in people with PDA. They may switch from one mood to another very suddenly in a way that can be described as "like switching a light on and off". To other people, the emotions can seem very dramatic and over the top, like an act, and there's sometimes no obvious reason. But this switching of mood can be in response to perceived pressure or a demand, and is driven by the need to control. It can make people with PDA very unpredictable. For most, this difficulty continues into adulthood.

People with a Demand Avoidant Profile, especially children, are often highly interested in role play and pretend, sometimes to an extreme extent. They will often use role play or pretend as part of a strategy to avoid demands or exercise control. When they become involved in play scenarios with other people, they will nearly always try to direct and this can cause real conflict, especially with other children and in later adult life.

This was recognised early on as being different from many other profiles as people with a Demand Avoidant Profile often mimic and take on the roles of others, extending and taking on their style, not simply repeating and re-enacting what they may have heard or seen in a repetitive or echoed way. About a third of children in early studies were reported to confuse reality and pretence at times. This is also the case for many people with other Autism behaviour profiles.

The large majority of children with a Demand Avoidant Profile are delayed in some aspect of their early speech and language development, although this may be dependent on their intellectual ability, and there is often a sudden degree of catch-up again this is very similar to Autism and Aspergers Syndrome traits. People with PDA profile have a more socially accepted use of eye contact (other than when avoiding demands) and conversational timing than others on the Autism Spectrum. Generally, they tend to have less difficulty understanding non verbal communication.

However, some do have difficulties such as taking things literally and understanding sarcasm and teasing. While the majority of people with a Demand Avoidant Profile become fluent in using expressive language, some have a problem with their understanding. They can have difficulty with processing what they hear and they need additional time to do this.

These difficulties may lead to misunderstanding and disruption to the communication process, which can contribute to their behaviour. Strong fascinations and special interests pursued to an 'obsessive' degree are very characteristic of people with all Autism profiles. However, Elizabeth Newson noted that the PDA behaviour itself usually has an 'obsessive feel'. People with a Demand Avoidant Profile may have a strong fascination with pretend characters and scenarios or real people they interact with. This can result in blame, victimisation and harassment that cause problems with peer relationships.

Just as in other Autism profiles, people with this profile can have difficulty processing everyday sensory information such as sound, sight, smell, taste, and touch. They can also have vestibular (balance) and proprioceptive (body awareness) difficulties. A large proportion of people with a Demand Avoidant Profile can have real problems controlling and regulating their emotions, particularly anger. As children, this can take the form of prolonged meltdowns as well as less dramatic avoidance strategies like distraction and giving excuses. It is essential to see this as extreme anxiety or 'panic attacks' and to treat them as such. Try using reassurance, calming strategies and de-escalation techniques.

Similar to others on the Autism Spectrum, the behaviour of a person with a Demand Avoidant Profile can vary between settings. For example, a child can appear very anxious at home, but calm at school. This is a learned coping strategy, and a lack of understanding of the real reasons for these differences can make parents feel very isolated and inadequate. In other cases, 'outbursts' are far worse at school, where demands may be much greater, and this can lead to multiple exclusions at an early age. For some children, this anxiety can develop to such an extent that they become school refusers.

As PDA is considered to be a behaviour profile within the Autism Spectrum, it is usually identified following a diagnostic assessment for Autism. This is usually by a multi disciplinary team made up of a combination of professionals including paediatricians, clinical and educational psychologists, psychiatrists, speech and language therapists and occupational therapists. Recognition of PDA as a behaviour profile within the Autism Spectrum is fairly recent, and the apparent social abilities of many people with this profile mask their problems. Many children are not identified until they are older and may already have been diagnosed with a different Autism profile. Sometimes parents may feel that this different profile doesn't quite fit. The surface sociability and the often vivid imaginations of children with a demand avoidant profile can confuse professionals making the diagnosis.

Other Autistic children and adults can display one or more of the behavioural features of PDA. When many occur together it is helpful to have an assessment because a diagnosis helps people with PDA and their families to understand why they experience certain difficulties and what they can do about them. It allows people to access services, support and appropriate advice about strategies avoids incorrect assumptions and diagnoses, such as Personality Disorder, Oppositional Defiance Disorder, Bi Polar, Borderline Personality Disorder, or ADHD. To begin the assessment process, ask your GP for a referral to a local paediatrician or AS specialist unit (if for you or your child) or team who specialise in Autism. The recognition of PDA and the skills in local teams to make an assessment may vary regionally. PDA is not currently recognised as a discrete diagnosis within national and international standards. The PDA Society also have information about the diagnostic pathway for children and adults.

A large number of people find that tried and tested strategies used with people who have other Autism profiles are not effective for people with a Demand Avoidant Profile. This is because people with this profile need a less directive and more flexible approach than others on the Autism Spectrum. Underpinning this approach is the understanding that a person with PDA does not make a deliberate choice to not comply and they can't overcome their need to be in control. However, with the right support, they may begin to make a series of achievements as trust and confidence builds.

One of the most common mistakes made by clinicians lacking Autism experience is to make a number of observations that don't take the issues related to Autism into account which can result in a misdiagnosis. Sometimes they may observe issues such as a person's clumsiness (possible dyspraxia), reading difficulty (possible dyslexia), poor attention span (possible Attention Deficit Disorder), difficulty with social communication (semantic pragmatic disorder or social communication disorder), mental health issues, or behavioural issues and diagnose that issue as the main condition. They may miss the fact that Autism is underlying the obvious difficulties seen on the surface and this can delay a more accurate diagnosis, delaying adequate help and support.

International Classification of Diseases, tenth edition (ICD-10) and Diagnostic and Statistical Manual (DSM-5).

The ICD-10 is the most commonly used diagnostic manual in the UK. It presents a number of possible Autism profiles, such as childhood Autism, Atypical Autism and Asperger Syndrome. These profiles are included under the Pervasive Developmental Disorders heading, defined as "A group of disorders characterised by qualitative abnormalities in reciprocal social interactions and in patterns of communication, and by a restricted, stereotyped, repetitive repertoire of interests and activities. These qualitative abnormalities are a pervasive feature of the individual's functioning in all situations".

A revised edition (ICD-11) is expected in late 2019 and is likely to closely align with the latest edition of the American Diagnostic and Statistical Manual (DSM), fifth edition (DSM-5) Although not the most commonly used manual in the UK, DSM-5 is likely to have a significant influence on the next edition of the ICD. This manual has recently been updated and is also used by diagnosticians. The diagnostic criteria are clearer and simpler than in the previous version of the DSM, and sensory behaviours are now included. This is useful as many Autistic people have sensory issues which affect them on a day to day basis. It now includes 'specifiers' to indicate support needs and other factors that impact on the diagnosis.

The manual defines Autism Spectrum disorder as "persistent difficulties with social communication and social interaction" and "restricted and repetitive patterns of behaviours, activities or interests" (this includes sensory behaviour), present since early childhood, to the extent that these "limit and impair everyday functioning".

In DSM-5, the terms 'Autistic disorder', 'Asperger disorder', 'childhood disintegrative disorder' and 'Pervasive Developmental Disorder - Not Otherwise Specified (PDD-NOS)' have been replaced by the collective term 'Autism Spectrum Disorder' (ASD). This means that it's likely that 'Autism Spectrum Disorder' (ASD) will become the most commonly given diagnosis. For many people, the term Asperger Syndrome is part of their day-to-day vocabulary and identity, so it is understandable that there are concerns around the removal from DMS-5 of Asperger Syndrome as a distinct category. Everyone who currently has a diagnosis on the Autism Spectrum, including those with Asperger Syndrome, will retain their diagnosis. No one will 'lose' their diagnosis because of the changes in DSM-5. Research has found that using the appropriate techniques, the new DSM-5 criteria correctly identified people and is reliable who should receive a diagnosis of ASD across age and ability. (Kent R.G. et al, 2013)

DSM-5 has introduced specifiers to help the clinician to describe associated or additional conditions, eg intellectual impairment, language impairment, genetic conditions, behavioural disorder, catatonia. One of the specifiers relates to the 'severity' of social communication impairments and restricted, repetitive patterns of behaviour. There are 3 levels: requiring support, requiring substantial support, requiring very substantial support. This can allow the clinician to give an indication of how much someone's condition affects them and how much support an individual needs. However, people who receive a diagnosis are not automatically eligible for support. DSM-5 explains that 'severity' levels may vary by context and also fluctuate over time, that the descriptive severity categories should not be used to determine eligibility for and provision of services, and that 'these can only be developed at an individual level and through discussion of personal priorities and targets'.

The DSM-5 now includes a condition called 'social communication disorder', separate to 'Autism Spectrum Disorder'. This would be given where someone exhibits social interaction and social communication difficulties and does not show restricted, repetitive patterns of behaviour, interests or activities. The DSM and ICD-10 criteria create the scope to use for diagnostic tools such as the DISCO (Diagnostic Interview for Social and Communication Disorders), the ADI-R (Autism Diagnostic Interview - Revised), and the ADOS (Autism Diagnostic Observation Schedule). These, and other diagnostic tools, are used to collect information in order to help to decide whether someone is on the Autism Spectrum or not. The criteria form the basis for the diagnosis, but the individual clinician's judgement is crucial.

The DISCO diagnostic tool does not rely on the algorithms for ICD-10 and DSM-5. The approach is dimensional rather than categorical. The DISCO not only gives a diagnosis but gives an understanding of the profile and needs including persistent difficulties with social communication and social interaction. Autistic people have difficulties with interpreting both verbal and non-verbal language like gestures or tone of voice. Many have a very literal understanding of language, and think people always mean exactly what they say. They may find it difficult to use or understand facial expressions, tone of voice, jokes and sarcasm. Some may not speak, or have fairly limited speech. They will often understand more of what other people say to them than they are able to express, yet may struggle with vagueness or abstract concepts. Some Autistic people benefit from using, or prefer to use, alternative means of communication, such as sign language or visual symbols. Some are able to communicate very effectively without speech.

Other Issues and Controversies

The exact cause of Autism is still being investigated. Research into causes suggests that a combination of factors genetic and environmental - may account for differences in development. Autism is not caused by a person's upbringing, or their social circumstances and is not the fault of the individual with the condition. There is no 'cure' for Autism. However, there is a range of strategies and approaches - methods of enabling learning and development - which people may find to be helpful.

Is there a link between Autism and Learning Disabilities? Around a third of people with a learning disability may also be Autistic, according to research published by Emerson and Baines in 2010. These studies described above identified Autism in children, the great majority of whom had learning disabilities and special educational needs.

However, in 1944, Hans Asperger in Vienna had published an account of children with many similarities to Kanner Autism but who had abilities, including grammatical language, in the average or superior range. There are continuing arguments concerning the exact relationship between Asperger and Kanner Syndromes but it is beyond dispute that they have in common the triad of impairments of social interaction, communication and imagination and a narrow, repetitive pattern of activities (Wing, 1981; 1991). Kanner's Syndrome is characterised by infantile Autism, with signs of lack of attachment, avoidance of eye contact, and general failure to develop social relationships; rituals and compulsive behaviour manifested by a resistance to change and repetitive acts; general intellectual retardation; and language disorders.

The definition of the term Atypical Autism (uncountable) An autism spectrum disorder that does not meet the diagnostic criteria for either Autism proper or Asperger's syndrome. Whereby Classic Autism - (also known as Autistic Disorder) is an Autism Spectrum Disorder (ASD). Is generally classified by impairment in social interactions and communication and includes some restrictive or repetitive behaviours.

Pervasive Developmental Disorder (PDD), As opposed to specific developmental disorders (SDD), is a group of five disorders characterised by delays in the development of multiple basic functions including socialisation and communication. The pervasive developmental disorders are: the four Autism Spectrum Disorders and Rett Syndrome. Rett Syndrome is much rarer, and is sometimes placed in the Autism Spectrum and sometimes not with more future research needed.

High-functioning Autism (HFA) is a term applied to people with Autism who do not have an Intellectual disability (An IQ of 70 or more) Individuals with HFA may exhibit deficits in areas of communication, emotion recognition and expression, and social interaction. HFA is not a recognized diagnosis in the DSM-5 or the ICD-10. Further differences in features between people with high-functioning autism and those with Asperger syndrome, include the following: People with HFA have a lower verbal reasoning ability, Better visual/spatial skills (higher performance IQ) than people with Asperger syndrome, Less deviating locomotion than people with Asperger syndrome People with HFA more often have problems functioning independently Curiosity and interest for many different things, in contrast to people with Asperger syndrome. People with Asperger syndrome are better at empathising with another. The male to female ratio of 4:1 for HFA is much smaller than that of Asperger syndrome. Individuals with Autism Spectrum disorders, including High-Functioning Autism, risk developing symptoms of anxiety. While anxiety is one of the most commonly occurring mental health symptoms, children and adolescents with High Functioning Autism are at an even greater risk of developing symptoms.

There are other comorbidities, the presence of one or more disorders in addition to the primary disorder, associated with HFA. including bipolar disorder and obsessive compulsive disorder (OCD). The link between HFA and OCD, has particularly been studied; both have abnormalities associated with serotonin levels of the brain other observable comorbidities associated with HFA include ADHD, Tourette Syndrome, and possibly criminal behaviour. While the association between HFA and criminal behaviour is not completely characterised, several studies have shown that the features associated with HFA correlates with an increased probability of engaging in criminal behaviour. While there is still a great deal of research that needs to be done in this area, recent studies suggest that there is a need to understand attributes of HFA that lead to violent behaviour. There have been several case studies that link the lack of empathy and social naïveté associated with HFA to criminal actions. HFA does not cause nor include intellectual disabilities, could a person with HFA have intellectual disabilities? This characteristic distinguishes HFA from the rest of the Autism Spectrum; between 40 and 55% of individuals with Autism have an intellectual disability.

Although little is known about the biological basis of Autism, some people refer to Autism as brain damage but perhaps in this book we prefer to say blind spot thinking and certainly some of the behaviours of a person on the Spectrum can reflect this.

Many autistic rights activists disagree with the categorisation of individuals into "High-functioning Autism" and "Low-functioning Autism", they argue that the "low-functioning" label causes people to put low expectations on a child and view them as lesser. Furthermore, critics of functioning labels state that an individual's functioning can fluctuate from day to day, and these categories do not take this into consideration.

There is a belief that some vaccinations, such as the MMR (measles, mumps, rubella) vaccine, may cause Autism. This was based on a research study published by Andrew Wakefield. The public information from the NHS believes the MMR is a safe and effective combined vaccine that protects against 3 separate illnesses - measles, mumps and rubella (German measles) - in a single injection. The full course of MMR vaccination requires 2 doses. Measles, mumps and rubella are highly infectious conditions that can have serious, potentially fatal complications, including meningitis, swelling of the brain (encephalitis) and deafness. They can also lead to complications in pregnancy that affect the unborn baby, and can lead to miscarriage. Since the MMR vaccine was introduced in 1988, it's rare for children in the UK to develop these serious conditions. But outbreaks can happen and there have been cases of measles in recent years, so it's important to make sure that you and your children are up-to-date with the MMR vaccination. The MMR vaccine is widely used around the world, with over 500 million doses having been given in over 100 countries as of 2001. Measles resulted in 2.6 million deaths per year before immunisation became common. This has decreased to 122,000 deaths per year as of 2012, mostly in low income countries. Through vaccination, as of 2018, rates of measles in North and South America are very low. Rates of disease have been seen to increase in populations which go unvaccinated. Between 2000 and 2016, vaccination decreased measles deaths by a further 84%. The results of Wakefield's study caused some parents to take their children off vaccines clinically proven to prevent diseases that can cause intellectual disabilities or death.

Why does Autism happen and can we actually fix it? We believe the answer to this is actually "No" as it is both environmental (due to the environment we live in changing our cell formation) and biological factors such as the fact that we have inherited the condition due to our genetic structures and makeup. Being on the Autism Spectrum is actually who we are as defined individuals and the science manuals of the DSM 5 and ICT 10 have yet to catch us up. We would further like to stress at this point as a note of guidance that anyone reading this that can identify with any characteristics or Autism (Phrenotype) may want to get a clinical diagnosis by a confirmed professional. If you cannot identify with some of the classified behaviours, over the next few chapters we will take a look at some of the unclassified behaviours, So now with the facts and clinical information out the way what are we actually looking for?

Chapter 3

What Are We Looking For?

Autism is a highly variable, neurodevelopmental disorder whose symptoms first appear after birth, during infancy or childhood, and generally follows a steady course without remission into later life. Early pioneers in bringing the condition to the forefront are Simon Baron Cohen, Tony Attwood, Temple Grandin, and Lorna Wing. There are countless others but ten years ago these people's perspectives were important to me when my son was newly diagnosed.

People with Autism may be severely impaired in some respects but normal, or even superior, in others. Symptoms gradually begin after the age of six months, become established by age two or three years and tend to continue through adulthood, although often in more muted form. Autism is distinguished not by a single symptom but by a characteristic triad of symptoms: impairments in social interaction; impairments in communication; and restricted interests and repetitive behaviour. Other aspects, such as atypical restricted or excessive eating, are also common but are not essential for diagnosis. Individual symptoms of Autism occur in the general population regardless of culture.

People with Autism have social impairments or deficits and often lack the intuition about others that many people take for granted. Unusual social development becomes apparent early in childhood. Autistic infants show less attention to social stimuli, smile and look at others less often, and respond less to their own name, or they could be the other end of the spectrum and be highly advanced in social communication above their own age. Autistic toddlers differ more strikingly from social norms; for example, they have less eye contact and turn-taking, and do not have the ability to use simple movements to express themselves, such as pointing at things. They can be less likely to exhibit social understanding, approach others spontaneously, imitate and respond to emotions, communicate nonverbally, and take turns with others. However, they do form attachments to their primary caregivers. Most children with Autism display moderately less attachment, although this difference disappears in children with higher mental development or less severe ASD. Older children and adults with ASD perform worse on tests of face and emotion recognition although this may be partly due to a lower ability to define their own emotions.

Children with high-functioning Autism suffer from more intense and frequent loneliness despite the common belief that children with Autism prefer to be alone. Making and maintaining friendships often proves to be difficult for those with Autism. For them, the quality of friendships, not the number of friends, predicts how lonely they feel. Functional friendships, such as those resulting in invitations to parties, may affect the quality of life more deeply.

There are many reports, but few studies, of aggression and violence in individuals with ASD. The limited data suggest that, in children with intellectual disability, Autism is associated with aggression, destruction of property, and meltdowns. About a third to a half of individuals with Autism do not develop enough natural speech to meet their daily communication needs. Differences in communication may be present from the first year of life, and may include delayed onset of babbling, unusual gestures, diminished responsiveness, and vocal patterns that are not synchronised with the caregiver. Children with autism are less likely to make requests or share experiences, and are more likely to simply repeat others' words (echolalia) or pronoun reversal when children or adults refer to themselves as he she or you or by the first name.

Autistic spectrum individuals can display many forms of repetitive or restricted behaviour, Stereotyped behaviours include repetitive movements, such as hand flapping, head rolling, or body rocking. These are compulsive behaviours: Time-consuming behaviours intended to reduce anxiety that an individual feels compelled to perform repeatedly or according to rigid rules, such as placing objects in a specific order, checking things, or hand washing. Where sameness is considered of high importance, there will be regulation, routine, resistance to change; for example, insisting that the furniture not be moved or refusing to be interrupted. Ritualistic behaviour encompasses an unvarying pattern of daily activities, such as an unchanging menu or a dressing ritual. This is closely associated with sameness. Restricted interests comprise interest or fixations that are abnormal in theme or intensity of focus, such as preoccupation with a single television program, toy, or game. Self-injury can include behaviours such as eye-poking, skin-picking, hand-biting and head-banging or self harm. No single repetitive or self-injurious behaviour seems to be specific to Autism, but Autism appears to have an elevated pattern of occurrence and severity of behaviours.

Autistic spectrum individuals may have symptoms that are independent of the diagnosis that can affect the individual or the family. An estimated 0.5% to 10% of individuals with ASD show unusual abilities, ranging from splinter skills such as the memorisation of trivia to the extraordinarily rare talents of prodigious Autistic savants eg: a specialism in mathematics, science, art, music or languages. Many individuals with ASD show superior skills in perception and attention, relative to the general population.

Sensory abnormalities are found in over 90% of those with Autism, and are considered core features by some, although there is no good evidence that sensory symptoms differentiate Autism from other developmental disorders. Differences are greater for under-responsivity (for example, walking into things) than for over-responsivity (for example, distress from loud noises) or for sensation seeking (for example, rhythmic movements).

An estimated 60–80% of Autistic spectrum people have motor signs that include poor muscle tone, poor motor planning, and toe walking;

deficits in motor coordination are pervasive across ASD and are great-er in Autism proper. At the other end of the scale they may be over achievers in sport with strong athletic tendencies.

Unusual eating behaviour occurs in about three-quarters of children or adults with ASD, to the extent that it was formerly a diagnostic indi-cator. Selectivity is the most common problem, although eating rituals and food refusal also occur along with allergies, sensitivities to certain foods for eg: celiac, dairy, peanut, or soya. Acid reflux in babies can be an earlier indicator to signs of food sensitivities intolerance or early dietary problems. GI Specialist Tim Buie raises care and concern of the autistic population with gastric problems on autism speaks about the issues.

Highly restrictive diets are common among people with autism. One client said as a toddler, she wouldn't eat anything but boiled eggs and bread with warm milk. At home, that wasn't a problem, but when she started primary school at age 4 and was required to eat the school's hot lunch, she refused. "These meals were so revolting that I developed a phobia of eating them," She says. She also found it stressful to eat in front of her classmates. "I would go the entire school day without food."

Anorexia is not the only eating disorder connected to autism. Al-though the majority of research on eating disorders in autism has been focused on people who routinely eat too little food, some women with autism may also turn to food for comfort. Some estimates hold that as much as 20 per cent of people with enduring eating disorders have autism. Recognising that someone has both autism and an eating dis-order is only the first step. Few psychologists have expertise in helping people who have both conditions. Some studies on autism and was struck by the similarities between the cognitive profiles of the two conditions. In particular, people with anorexia struggle to recognise the impact of their behaviour on others. "They can be very empathic and have a great desire to be accepted by other people, but they also seem a bit impervious to how their starvation affects others," In that sense, people with anorexia seem a lot like those with autism. People with anorexia often have difficulties making friends and sustaining social relationships even before the onset of their condition. People with anorexia or eating disorders it is well documented that they have rigid patterns of thinking and behaviour, an insistence on control, sameness and difficulty with change, all of which are commonly seen in people with autism.

ASD individuals have higher levels of stress. Siblings of people with ASD report greater admiration of and less conflict with the affected sibling ASD is also common amongst other siblings who often display either similar character traits or diverse opposite character traits. There is tentative evidence that Autism occurs more frequently in people with gender dysphoria. Gastrointestinal problems are one of the most commonly associated medical disorders in people with Autism. These are linked to greater social impairment, irritability, behaviour and sleep problems, language impairments and mood changes, anxiety, depression, and phobias are all considered common behaviours.

Through our own personal learning journey of Autism and Asperger's Syndrome and the countless books we may read on the subject and the personalities we come across, context blindness does play a huge critical aspect to an Autism brain. Context blindness can best be described as a harmonious orchestra where you have a group of wind instruments of clarinet and flute players, the percussion family and the woodwind family who all play harmoniously, one particular section and one particular violin player is missing a beat and playing off key. Only the conductor would notice that the violin is off beat. If you apply this theory to the actual human brain where all other parts are working well but one small part is perhaps playing a tune to the wrong beat, this can best be described as a form of context blindness that people on the Autism Spectrum actually have. You could also look at it as a form of faulty wiring or a wiring connection that differs from everyone else, where your one particular instrument is playing at a different pace. This can take form in the way of denial, slow processing, lack of self awareness, not getting or understanding facial expressions, missing emotions, being overly empathetic, negative behaviours, tics, flapping, or black and white thinking in general with no shades of grey in between. These are a few examples of how context blindness can be in context. This is where subconsciously all the warning signs are there but we Aspies chose to ignore them and continue to repeat patterns of behaviour regardless of the same outcomes, because it becomes familiar to us as that warm feeling of comfort of similar repeated behaviours.

On our journey of discovery we began to question the link between Autism, and difficulty mastering certain things, which can stem from Pervasive Developmental disorders. The diagnostic category of Pervasive Developmental disorders (PDD) refers to a group of disorders characterised by delays in the development of socialisation and communication skills. Symptoms are apparent as early as infancy, although the typical age of onset is before 3 years of age. Symptoms may include problems with using and understanding language; difficulty relating to people, objects, and events; unusual play with toys and other objects; difficulty in give and take as adult ie: not sharing or maintaining a 50/50 relationship or interaction where it is all one sided interaction, difficulty with changes in routine or familiar surroundings, and repetitive body movements or behaviour patterns. Autism (a developmental brain disorder characterised by impaired social interaction and communication skills, and a limited range of activities and interests) is the most characteristic and best studied PDD (Pathological Demand Disorder and or PDA Pathological Demand Avoidance).

Autism is a psychological construct that may exist separately as Autistic at the moment Science has yet to identify if it is responsive to other factors for example people whose behaviour has changed to illness, brain inflammation, coma, car accident etc. Because of the changes in the brain their personalities have changed to become more autistic in many of their behaviours that did not exist before the illness or accident. So from our understanding it can be very difficult for the loved one's partner to cope with the changes in the persons personality and many often say they do not get the same person back that they had before the accident or illness.

People with PDA vary widely in ability, intelligence, and behaviours. Some people do not speak at all, others speak in limited phrases or conversations, and some have relatively normal language development. Repetitive skills and limited social skills are generally evident. Unusual responses to sensory information, such as loud noises, not being able to distinguish between hot and cold temperatures and lights, are also common. People with Autism Spectrum Disorders may have trouble communicating, reading body language, learning basic skills, making friends, and making eye contact many have the learning difficulties of dyslexia, dyspraxia, dysphasia, auditory and visual processing problems.

OCD, gambling, drug abuse, alcohol misuse, eating disorders anorexia, and bulmenia become ingrained personality traits as addictive patterns of mental behaviour. Addiction and substance misuse is common in people with mental health problems according to reports published in the Journal of the American Medical Association. Roughly 50 per cent of individuals with severe mental disorders are affected by substance abuse. 37 per cent of alcohol abusers and 53 per cent of drug abusers also have at least one serious mental illness. Of all people diagnosed as mentally ill, 29 per cent abuse either alcohol or drugs. Source: National Alliance on Mental Illness.

So with these figures does that mean that 1/3 of us at any given time are mentally ill suffering severe anxiety, depression and substance abusing to cope? Or is a certain type of behaviour not yet categorised in the DSM Manual as a form of Autism, for example, hoarding behaviour, agoraphobia, eating disorders, or a compulsive or controlling behaviour.

A Compulsive behaviour is defined as performing an act persistently and repetitively without it necessarily leading to an actual reward or pleasure. Compulsive behaviours could be an attempt to make obsessions go away. The act could be a small, restricted and repetitive behaviour, yet not disturbing in a pathological way. Compulsive behaviours are a need to reduce apprehension caused by internal feelings a person wants to abstain from or control. A major cause of the compulsive behaviours is said to be obsessive–compulsive disorder (OCD). "The main idea of compulsive behaviour is that the likely excessive activity is not connected to the purpose to which it appears directed. Furthermore, there are many different types of compulsive behaviours including, shopping, hoarding, eating, gambling, trichotillomania and picking skin, checking, counting, washing, sex addiction, lying and more. Also, there are cultural examples of compulsive behaviour for example excessive praying, obsessing over certain parts or passages of bible and a compulsion to excessively stick to it word for word.

About 50 million people in the world today appear to suffer from some type of obsessive-compulsive disorder. Sufferers are often more secretive than other people with psychological problems, so the more serious psychological disorders are diagnosed more often. Many who exhibit compulsive behaviour will claim it is not a problem and may endure the condition for years before seeking help.

The main types include but are not exclusive to Addiction as Addiction is simply a compulsion toward a rewarding stimulus. Behavioural Addictions, are sometimes referred to as impulse control disorders, are increasingly recognised as treatable forms of addiction. The type of excessive behaviours identified as being addictive include gambling, food, sexual intercourse, use of pornography, stalking, use of computers, playing video games, use of the internet, exercise and drugs but this list is by no means exhaustive. Many people may be addicted to many different and unusual things, where it stems from is the Autistic brains obsessive compulsion with a specific thing, place or object. Some obsessions are healthier life choices than others but become the Autistic special interest and focus where anxiety and depression does set in if the need is not met. What we are suggesting here is to avoid the impression of conflating symptoms, over engaging people in a dramatic diagnostic inflation that could lead too easily to a tick box assessment.

Perfectionism is not about being obsessed with perfection. It's an unhealthy need to do things perfectly, appear perfect, and have perfection surround you. Perfectionism is driven by fear: fear of making mistakes, fear of disapproval, and fear of not meeting impossible standards and unattainable goals, all to avoid or minimise shame, blame, and judgment which can also be self-inflicted. Perfectionism is strongly linked to depression, anxiety, and other disorders, because it makes the person feel like they are never good enough. The perfectionist, will beat themselves up for not getting things exactly right.

Perfectionism is very common among people & children with autism. As the name implies, perfectionists are driven to do everything perfectly. Logically they know no one is perfect, however, when they make a mistake or perceive that they have 'failed' they emotionally beat themselves up verbally, physically or mentally saying things like "I'm so stupid/ useless/ hopeless/ incompetent. I can't do anything right." Perfectionism can be both a good and a bad thing: those who have it are often very hard workers and put their best effort into everything they do. But this comes at the high cost of their mental and sometimes physical wellbeing & health.

There are several factors that cause perfectionism in people with autism. Here are just a few of them: Black and White/All or Nothing Thinking: Common to typical perfectionists, many perfectionists on the spectrum, tend to feel that their work is either perfect or dreadful, with nothing in between. So, they think that they are either succeeding or failing at any given task. This black and white thinking is the cause of their anxiety and distress. Attention to Detail: When people are extremely attention to detail oriented, they are naturally going to be more likely to notice even the tiniest errors, spelling mistakes or flaws. Social Issues: Many perfectionists feel that people will only love them or view them as having worth if they do everything right. This may also be the case for children with autism. A child on the spectrum who struggles with social cues may not know what their peers are thinking or feeling when they make a mistake so it causes them high anxiety & stress.

Perseveration: Children with autism often get "stuck" on certain repetitive thoughts. As a result, they may be unable to stop thinking about whatever mistake they may have made, which fuels anxiety about making future mistakes. Communication Difficulties: If children have trouble knowing how to ask for help because they struggle with communication, that makes failure even more stressful because how do they get help if they don't know how to ask for it?

Many of those character personality traits have yet to be linked to Autism as Science is not that yet advanced however these are the everyday problems people have difficulty coping with. It is our view from the scores of people who have sought professional help for their perfectionism, addictive impulse based or OCD behaviour or the need for control it is linked to ADHD - Attention Deficit Hyper Activity Disorder where the mind, due to faulty wiring is craving an impulse to act out to quell or quash the demand inside. This flow of consciousness is almost confabulation.

ADHD has three types of symptoms, each type of ADHD is tied to one or more characteristics. ADHD is characterised by inattention and hyperactive-impulsive behaviour. These behaviours often present in the following ways:

Inattention - getting distracted, having poor concentration and organisational skills. Impulsivity - interrupting, taking risks. Hyperactivity - never seeming to slow down, talking and fidgeting, difficulties staying on task. Everyone is different, so it's common for two people to experience the same symptoms in different ways. For example, these behaviours are often different in boys and girls. Boys may be seen as more hyperactive, and girls may be quietly inattentive.

Predominantly inattentive ADHD If you have this type of ADHD, you may experience more symptoms of inattention than those of impulsivity and hyperactivity. You may struggle with impulse control or hyperactivity at times. But these aren't the main characteristics of inattentive ADHD. People who experience inattentive behaviour often, miss details and are distracted easily get bored quickly, have trouble focusing on a single task, have difficulty organising thoughts and learning new information, lose pencils, papers, or other items needed to complete a task, don't seem to listen, move slowly and appear as if they're daydreaming, process information more slowly and less accurately than others, have trouble following directions. More girls are diagnosed with inattentive type ADHD than boys.

Predominantly hyperactive-impulsive ADHD, This type of ADHD is characterised by symptoms of impulsivity and hyperactivity. People with this type can display signs of inattention, but it's not as marked as the other symptoms. People who are impulsive or hyperactive often, squirm, fidget, or feel restless, have difficulty sitting still, talk constantly, touch and play with objects, even when inappropriate to the task at hand, have trouble engaging in quiet activities, are constantly "on the go", are impatient, act out of turn and don't think about consequences of actions, blurt out answers and inappropriate comments. Children or adults with hyperactive-impulsive type ADHD can be a disruption in the classroom or work setting. They can make learning more difficult for themselves and other students/colleagues. Combination ADHD If you have the combination type, it means that your symptoms don't exclusively fall within the inattention or hyperactive-impulsive behaviour. Instead, a combination of symptoms from both of the categories are exhibited. Most people, with or without ADHD, experience some degree of inattentive or impulsive behaviour. But it's more severe in people with ADHD. The behaviour occurs more often and interferes with how you function at home, school, work, and in social situations.

In 2016 new research supported evidence by Epilepsy Research UK that people with epilepsy are at an increased risk of developing autism spectrum disorder (ASD), especially if their epilepsy begins in childhood. (Personally I believe that people with ASD can have Epilepsy and Epilepsy is a component of the Autistic Spectrum so anyone who has the condition will also display AS traits). The study, published in the journal Neurology, also indicates that ASD is more common than usual in the siblings and offspring of people with epilepsy. Epilepsy has many causes, some of which affect a tiny area of the brain.

These findings suggest that it could be so for some at least with epilepsy and their family members for ASD, so that they can receive prompt and optimal care. The increased risk of epilepsy in people with ASD, and especially in those with additional learning disabilities, however, only recently have researchers begun to explore the risk of ASD in people with epilepsy from Epilepsy Research UK.

A study, carried out at University Hospital in Linköping, Sweden, used the Swedish Patient Registry to identify more than 85,000 people with epilepsy and their siblings and children. For each of the 85,000 people with epilepsy, they selected five other people of the same age and sex, and who lived in the same county, but did not have epilepsy (controls). These were used for comparison and their siblings and children were also identified taking into consideration confounding socio economic variables.

The scientists used the data available in the registry to find out what proportion of people in each group (people with epilepsy and controls) had been diagnosed with ASD. They then did a comparison of the ASD rates in the siblings and children of people with epilepsy, and the ASD rates in the siblings and children of controls.

The findings showed that 1,381/85,000 people with epilepsy (or 1.6%) also had a diagnosis of ASD, compared to 700/425,000 (or 0.2%) of controls. This is an eight-fold increase. The researchers conclude from this that people with epilepsy have a significantly increased risk of developing ASD. Their results also suggested that the highest risk of ASD is in people who develop epilepsy in childhood.

Focusing on the siblings and children, the team found that those of people with epilepsy also had a higher risk than normal of developing ASD than those of controls, although it was still relatively low. For the children of parents with epilepsy, the risk was shown to be higher if it was the mother who had epilepsy rather than the father, and the researchers speculate that this may be a result of exposure to antiepileptic drugs in the womb. The exact mechanisms by which these two conditions are linked are not known. Earlier research has suggested a shared genetic basis, and the current study supports this view or is it merely consistent with that view.

Prevalence of epilepsy in children with autism Tuchman and Rapin (2002) found that the incidence of epilepsy in children with Autism ranged from 5% to 40%. Hughes and Melyn (2005) reported that the electroencephalographs (EEGs) of 75% of the children with autism showed abnormal patterns of electrical activity in the brain and 46% had seizures.

People with Autism who have epilepsy show different types of seizure. The figures vary because each person with autism and epilepsy has a different mixture of epileptic entities, some of which include seizures while others do not. This means that a better understanding of the relationship between epilepsy and ASD could help the development of new therapies that treat them both. In the meantime, health professionals need to be made aware of these findings, so that they can manage the combined conditions more effectively. Lead author, Dr Heléne Sundelin, comments: "The risk of autism for siblings and children to individuals with epilepsy are, despite the increase, still rather low. These results are more important for the understanding of the relationship between the disorders".

A child's risk of autism is also slightly elevated if one parent has asthma, according to a study of nearly 23,000 autistic children in Sweden. Children also have increased odds of autism if their mother is diagnosed with an autoimmune disease, according to another study, conducted in Finland.

Overall, the findings mesh with those of a 2005 study suggesting mothers who have asthma or allergies during the second trimester have more than double the typical risk of having a child with autism.

This interesting association deserves follow up, but it is by no means conclusive and further research needs to be done to determine this. As

Asthma can be stress or allergy related. 20 per cent of autistic children have mothers with asthma, compared with 14.3 per cent of children in the general population, the researchers found and that the autism risk is from the actual asthma itself and the immune reaction going on rather than the medication they are taking. Researchers also found an association between autism in a child and asthma or autoimmune conditions in the mother that involve inflammation of the eye or ear. For instance, asthma in mothers is associated with a 40 per cent increase in the odds of autism in the children. The researchers also found an increase in autism odds for children whose siblings have an autoimmune disease or who have one themselves.

Many people on the AS Spectrum may have a specialist skill or ability that defines normal capabilities, usually the skill or interest will fall in one of these eight areas - mathematic, science, languages, art/creativity, business, sport music or writing. More often than not the special interest or skill could lie in two areas or more but which ever area it lies in you can hazard a guess that this will be the autistics probably chosen profession for example a person with a keen interest in biology may become a scientist, a person with a natural flair for mathematics may become an accountant, a person with an skill in languages becomes a linguist, a musical ear, a visual designer and so on. It's by tapping into their natural autistic ability their special interest that they become a prodigy in their chosen subject because they find it a natural ability. In extreme cases ability can become exceptional and prestigious AS people can be singled out in their chosen specialism.

Some people on the Spectrum may have a tone of voice that is pitched higher or lower than the norm, or a tone that is slightly different or irritating. One such attempt is a new technology that analyses the nuances in peoples' voices, based on characteristics such as tone, pauses, press, and intonation, through a process known as 'machine learning method. It has 70 to 96 per cent accuracy" the Interacting Minds Centre Study and at the School of Communication and Culture, Aarhus University, Denmark shows that voice and prosody are potentially rich indicators of cognitive and clinical features, and could support clinicians in the screening and diagnostic process of Autism as many people with Autism lack the ability to use prosody and have what is often described as a "flat" voice. This is sometimes misinterpreted as a lack of interest, lack of intelligence, lack of humour, or lack of emotional response. However this one characteristic is not a pre requisite there has to be diagnostic tests for numerous characteristics.

Tourette syndrome is a neurological disorder as yet to be fully linked with autism. It causes repeated, involuntary physical movements and vocal outbursts. Tourette syndrome is an inherited neurological disorder with onset in childhood, characterised by the presence of multiple physical (motor) tics and at least one vocal tic; these tics characteristically wax and wane.

It is sometimes a co-morbid disorder with Autism Spectrum Disorders such as Autism and Asperger's syndrome. Tourette syndrome is the most severe kind of tic syndrome. Tics are involuntary muscle spasms. They consist of abrupt intermittent twitches of a group of muscles. The most frequent forms of tics involve: blinking, sniffing, grunting, throat clearing, grimacing, shoulder movements, head movements. As many as 1 in 100 experience milder symptoms.

The syndrome affects males nearly four times more than females. Symptoms can vary from one person to another. They usually appear between the ages of 3 and 9, starting with small muscle tics in your head and neck. Eventually, other tics may appear in your trunk and limbs. People diagnosed with Tourette syndrome often have both a motor tic and a vocal tic. The symptoms tend to worsen during periods of excitement, stress, or anxiety. They're generally most severe during your late teen years.

According to the Mayo Clinic, tics are classified by type, as in motor or vocal. Further classification includes simple or complex tics. Simple tics involve only one muscle group and are brief. Complex tics are co-ordinated patterns of movements or vocalisations that involve several muscle groups. Motor tics include simple motor tics and complex motor tics, eye blinking, smelling or touching objects, eye darting, making obscene gestures, sticking the tongue out bending or twisting your body, nose twitching, stepping in certain patterns, mouth movements, hopping, head jerking, shoulder shrugging. Vocal tics, include hiccupping, repeating your own words or phrases, grunting, repeating other people's words or phrases, coughing using vulgar or obscene words, throat clearing and barking.

Tourette is a highly complex syndrome. It involves abnormalities in various parts of your brain and the electrical circuits that connect them. An abnormality may exist in your basal ganglia, the part of your brain that contributes to your control of motor movements. Chemicals in your brain that transmit nerve impulses may also be involved. These chemicals are known as neurotransmitters. They include dopamine, serotonin, and norepinephrine. The cause of Tourette is unknown and there's no way to prevent it. Researchers believe that an inherited genetic defect may be the cause. But they have yet to identify the specific genes directly related to Tourette. Still, family clusters have been identified. These clusters lead researchers to believe that genetics play a role for some people with Tourettes. If we could include Tourettes as part of the AS Spectrum where exactly did it all originate from?

The vagueness of the border between able and disabled has made Asperger's controversial from the time it was coined as a diagnosis, in 1981, by English psychiatrist Lorna Wing. Wing named it after Hans Asperger, a Viennese paediatrician who in a 1944 paper had described four boys as sharing "a lack of empathy, little ability to form friendships, one-sided conversations, intense absorption in a special interest, and clumsy movements." He called them "little professors." (Asperger himself seems to have been a bit spectrum-y as a child, endlessly reciting the verse of Austrian poet Franz Grillparzer, to his classmates' dismay.) By 1990, Asperger's Syndrome was in common usage among clinicians as a term to describe a distinct verbal subset of Autistics. But exactly how Asperger's made it into the DSM-IV, published in 1994, remains veiled in mystery.

The recent publication of "In a Different Key" by John Donvan and Caren Zucker has revived accounts of historical precedents of Autism in feral children. This idea was borne out of Uta Frith's book "Autism: Explaining the Enigma" where she details the case of Victor of Aveyron. Victor was a young boy found living in the woods near Saint-Sernin-sur-Rance at about the age of 12. Although Victor could hear he lacked speech and communication skills. Victor had numerous scars in his body, preferred to eat raw meat, and would frolic nude in the snow all suggesting that he had been in the wild most of his life. Despite vigorous attempts at socialisation and education Victor only made rudimentary progress. Feral (or wild) children are those who live isolated from human contact since an early age. They have been a popular source for myths dating back thousands of years. Romulus and Remus, the twin brothers who presumably founded Rome, were raised by a she-wolf. More recently, the fictional character Tarzan (the Viscount of Greystoke) was raised by the Madgani great apes. In these mythical accounts, feral children are romanticised as noble savages often having superior intelligence and superior morals than children raised under the corrupting or "unnatural" influence of civilisation. Victor and other feral children do share some symptoms characteristic of Autism. They often fail to socialise appropriately, lack attention and spend time rocking themselves back and forth. Stereotypes in feral children are reminiscent of repetitive behaviours observed in caged or otherwise confined animals. Many of these repetitive movements have been used in research as animal models of anxiety and depression in humans.

However in Autism, stereotypes are often acquired early in life where they tend to be rigid, invariant, and inappropriate in nature. When stereotypes provide for self-stimulatory behaviours they are difficult to change regardless of environmental manipulations. Is this about stereotypes or about stereotypic behaviour as a psychological construct? This does not appear to be the case for caged animals. Rocking, swimming in circles, self-mutilation, can many times be treated in animals by environmental enrichment. Feral children do seem capable of establishing social reciprocity and empathy with those in their immediate surrounding. Although labelled as severely mentally impaired they must have displayed a great deal of practical intelligence and even theory of mind (e.g., towards other animals), for how else would they have been able to survive in the wild, even though other animals possess theory of mind according to some researchers.

In Autism the skills necessary to understand the emotions of others are sometimes impaired. Many Autistic individuals find it difficult to read gestures and body language. In Autism, although some individuals have delays in acquiring language many others do not (Asperger). For those who can't use spoken language sometimes they can be taught to communicate with written or typed language, American Sign Language, picture cards or digital communication devices. This ability to learn can be made apparent even after many years of being nonverbal. This does not seem to be the case for feral children. Although feral children do display some signs of Autism further speculations and assertions should be carefully considered.

The history of psychiatry is a long fade-in, a glacial zoom toward granularity. Autism emerged from a conceptual catchall called "childhood schizophrenia," especially in the USA and Asperger's, in turn, was carved out of Autism. But the more fine-grained the distinctions, the more they threaten to overlap and blur into each other. The community of clinicians specialising in developmental neurology generally viewed DSM-IIIR, which had been published in 1987, as wildly over inclusive. It had only two categories of spectrum disorders - Autism and the kitchen sink PDD-NOS (pervasive developmental disorder not otherwise specified) and its imprecision was seen as having led to an alarming increase in the number of diagnoses. The overarching agenda of DSM-IV, then, was to be more specific and to raise the bar for diagnosis. By the early nineties, the committee tasked with revising the taxonomy was focusing on whether Asperger's was fundamentally different from high functioning Autism. But their work was conscribed to hashing out the pros and cons of creating a separate diagnosis for Asperger's and didn't extend to making a decision or establishing what the diagnostic criteria would be. That work would fall to non specialist higher ups at the APA. Even as the committee finished several years' work, its members had no idea whether Asperger's would make it into the big book. "It was like the election of the Pope," says Peter Szatmari, a leading Canadian researcher who sat on the working group. "The message went upstairs, and we waited around for smoke to come out of the Vatican. And there it was."

The publication of DSM-IV had unintended consequences. "We were glad that Asperger's was included," says psychologist Bryna Siegel, another working-group member, who directs clinical care at the Autism clinic at the University of California, San Francisco, "but until the publication of DSM-IV, very few people had heard the term Asperger's. And when it came out, a lot of clinicians let their fingers do the walking in DSM. There were fully trained practicing clinicians who really didn't have any idea what Asperger's was. Everybody with Asperger's got diagnosed with Asperger's, but a lot of other people got diagnosed with Asperger's, too."

Because Asperger's lives on the outskirts of normal, and because its symptoms can resemble will fully antisocial behaviour, there's now a presumption of excuse making whenever someone invokes it to get out of a pickle. South Park aired an episode in which the people at an Asperger's group therapy centre turn out to be faking their symptoms and not even to believe in the reality of the disorder. (Cartman, meanwhile, mishearing Asperger's as "Ass Burgers," tries to fake it by stuffing his underwear with hamburgers.) "You're not Autistic," a doctor tells Hugh Laurie's abrasive character in an episode of House. "You don't even have Asperger's. You wish you did; it would exempt you from the rules, give you freedom, absolve you of responsibility, let you date 17-year-olds. But, most important, it would mean that you're not just a jerk."

Environmental risk factors for are the experiences of an individual during their lifetime that interact with the individual's genetic composition to increase or decrease his or her vulnerability to Autism. A number of different environmental factors have been implicated as risk factors, including various psychosocial stressors. Adverse childhood experiences (ACEs) are various forms of maltreatment and household dysfunction experienced in childhood. The Adverse Childhood Experiences Study by the Centres for Disease Control and Prevention has shown a strong dose–response relationship between ACEs and numerous health, social, and behavioural problems throughout a person's lifespan. Children's neurological development can be permanently disrupted when they are chronically exposed to stressful events such as physical, emotional, or sexual abuse, physical or emotional neglect, witnessing violence in the household, or a parent being incarcerated or suffering from a mental illness. As a result, the child's cognitive functioning or ability to cope with negative or disruptive emotions may be impaired. Over time, the child may adopt poor coping mechanisms, particularly during adolescence. Depression and Anxiety are the top layer of feelings that a person could feel about their condition but I will discuss more on this later in Chapter 4 where we will also look at the range of personalities.

Chapter 4

Anxiety and Depression

Many people suffer from anxiety and depression but what they don't realise is that anxiety is the surface result of why a person feels uneasy within themselves. Anxiety is the result of why a person feels uneasy but may not know what the underlying cause is.

People with anxiety disorders frequently have intense, excessive and persistent worry and fear about everyday situations. Often, anxiety disorders involve repeated episodes of sudden feelings of intense anxiety and fear or terror that reach a peak within minutes (panic attacks). In Autism a person who suffers with regular anxiety may not know or fully understand that the build up of the anxiety can result in panic attacks.

I have found through my work in Autism people may suffer increased levels of anxiety and stress because of interpersonal isolation. They feel different from other people and worry that they may be disliked or misunderstood. This may lead the child or adult with Autism to withdraw or avoid. This lack of contact with others can lead to more awkwardness and lack of opportunities to practice social interactions.

Those with Autism frequently report hypersensitivity to loud noises, touch, lights or other forms of sensation. When in situations that involve these areas of oversensitivity, they may also experience periods of stress and discomfort. Stress may again result in avoidance of places in which over-stimulation may occur. Furthermore, people with Autism may have trouble understanding the perspective of others. They may misinterpret communications and subtle interpersonal cues. These misunderstanding can lead to anxiety, worry, and difficulties in relationships. Withdrawal, rejection, or avoidance are natural reactions. Fear and worry can become worse and can build up which can be and usually is the top layer of anxiety; and individuals might not actually know what it is they are experiencing. They just know they are having symptoms of anxiety but have not connected what anxiety actually feels like.

The symptoms of anxiety depend on the type of anxiety disorder, but general symptoms include: Feelings of panic, fear, and uneasiness, problems sleeping, cold or sweaty hands or feet, shortness of breath, heart palpitations, not being able to be still and calm, dry mouth, feeling sick or queezy, numbness, difficulty concentrating, thinking constantly about the worst outcome, difficulty sleeping becoming preoccupied with or obsessive about one subject, perfectionism, flash backs, self consciousness, chronic indigestion, and muscle tensions. This list is not exhaustive and sometimes other symptoms may become systematic to the individual depending on the underlying cause of the anxiety or the fear that is lying underneath. Sometimes the Anxiety can manifest itself into a phobia if left to develop long enough without looking and identifying its root cause.

People with Autism who need structure, regularity and routine sometimes find it harder to think themselves out of an Anxiety driven mind set, because of the lack of theory of mind as mentioned in previous chapters, and coupled with context blindness, this is why Anxiety can take a hold.

For example an Autism client of mine had panic attacks around social situations involving food. She had developed an eating disorder and was extremely skinny. She refused to eat as it made her feel sick, and she was becoming depressed about the situation as she didn't understand what the root cause actually was. Anxiety had developed around any social situation that involved eating. After a couple of sessions she discovered that she had an underlying fear about not being in control and when control was taken away from her, (she had recently had a baby and as we know, all new born babies do not establish a routine over night) her anxiety had manifested itself in food. It was the one thing she could control about herself was how much she did and did not eat. My client's new born baby had taken away the element of control from her orderly life; and she was finding it difficult because there was little routine; and the baby was in control, demanding of her time. Her Anxiety had taken hold because she felt powerless about her situation, but could not see a way out or the reasons why it had developed in the first place. Once she understood she had felt out of control as a child and she was now the mother of a baby with little routine she was able to reduce her anxiety levels by taking control of her life back and gaining some sort of order.

Anxiety can be understood as growing out of a process or cycle. First there is something feared which results in distress. Avoidance temporarily brings down the feelings of distress and thus feels good. This good feeling is rewarding and results in more avoidance. The next time fear is experienced, there is a strong desire for avoidance. Thus fear grows and avoidance is the natural pathway. People with Anxiety and Autism can learn to slowly become exposed to what they fear, just like those with generalised Anxiety Disorder, Panic Disorder, or Obsessive Compulsive Disorder. They need a large dose of Cognitive Behaviour therapy from an understanding therapist.

Anxiety is one of the biggest challenges facing individuals on the Autism Spectrum. Parents and therapists and other professionals all want and need to know how to effectively manage feelings of Anxiety in individuals with Autism. While Anxiety and Autism seem to go hand in hand, there are relatively few resources that help manage these emotions. Anyone who has experienced Anxiety knows how debilitating it can be -- it affects us at work and home, interferes with sleep, affects our appetite, and can make daily activities a challenge. For individuals with Autism, Anxiety often impacts family, social, and academic life, which adds to the additional difficulties associated with Autism. Many poor coping methods can spring up as a result to manage Anxiety. These can include - comfort eating, smoking, drinking, drug taking, repetitive behaviours and OCD. All mask the underlying feelings and can help the individual feel temporarily better about a situation but they are not long term solutions and are often very unhealthy coping mechanisms.

People with Autism often struggle with social situations -- knowing what to say, how to use eye contact, using appropriate body language, and initiating conversations. Thus, individuals with Autism are much more likely to be Anxious about their social abilities and in certain individuals Anxiety can be more apparent especially those on the Autism Spectrum who have PDA (Pathological Demand Avoidance).

People with Autism also typically utilise "black and white" thinking, meaning they have trouble accepting exceptions to rules or beliefs or difficulty integrating new information that is outside of their own viewpoint and perspective. Emotional regulation is a third cause of Anxiety in individuals with Autism. When individuals with Autism react to a situation, it is often with extreme emotions. When they feel anxiety, individuals with Autism really experience that emotion, and it is often severe. People with Autism also often have more trouble identifying triggers and appropriate responses to these anxiety-causing situations.

While Anxiety and Autism are so closely linked, many parents would say that the subject of Anxiety reducing techniques was not a pressing issue when their child was first diagnosed. Therapy might include behavioural, occupational, speech, and other early interventions, but Anxiety management is often overlooked. While it might be unrealistic to think Anxiety will go away completely, it can be greatly diminished, and individuals with Autism can learn techniques for managing Anxiety and utilise these practices for themselves, which improves overall independence.

One huge trigger for individuals with Autism is change. Changing a routine or environment can have an extreme impact on a person with Autism. Some techniques for decreasing anxiety (and the tantrums, anger, stress, and other emotions associated with it) include discussing the change and using social stories. Helping a person with Autism really understand what is happening can help them prepare for the change. Social stories include pictures and often audio that will explain a scenario, and they give that black and white depiction of an event that people with Autism can understand more easily. The more you introduce a possible reward to a person with Autism, the more likely they are to accept, understand, and respond appropriately. Plenty of positive reinforcement should be given.

Does everyone have Anxiety and does that mean everyone has Autism or is on the Spectrum? Yes, we believe that because now a days we are more able to recognise what the symptoms of Anxiety actually are. Everyone gets worried or anxious from time to time - when speaking in public, for instance, or when going through financial difficulty. For some people, however, anxiety becomes so frequent, or so forceful, that it begins to take over their lives. Worry is problematic "when it creates chronically anxious thoughts, a depressed attitude, or feelings of being immobilised," So how can you tell if your everyday worry and anxiety has crossed the line? It's not easy. Anxiety disorders come in many different forms - such as anxiety attacks, phobia, and social anxiety - and the distinction between an official diagnosis and "normal" anxiety isn't always clear. So If you experience any of the symptoms on a regular basis, you may want to talk with your doctor or seek help from a therapist.

People are often unclear about the differences between anxiety and depression, and confused as to which is their primary problem. Here's an explanation of the differences between anxiety and depression, and some comments on the recovery process. However, as always, if you have the troubles described in this chapter, you are well advised to discuss these problems with a professional therapist.

Anxiety Disorders are characterised by a sense of doubt and vulnerability about future events. The attention of anxious people is focused on their future prospects, and the fear that those future prospects will be bad. Anxiety Disorders are characterised by a variety of symptoms involving anxious thoughts, unexplained physical sensations, and avoidant or self protective behaviours. People are often unclear about the differences between Anxiety and Depression, and confused as to which is their primary problem. I find this a useful explanation of the differences between Anxiety and Depression. A person whose primary problem is Depression, rather than Anxiety, generally doesn't show the same fear and uncertainty that people do with Anxiety Disorders. Depressed people are not so preoccupied with worrying about what might happen to them in the future. They think they already know what will happen, and they believe it will be bad. The same bad stuff that's happening to them now, the key symptoms of depression include: Feeling sad, and/or hopeless, lack of interest and enjoyment in activities that used to be fun and interesting, physical aches and pains without physical cause; lack of energy, difficulty concentrating, remembering, and/or making decisions, changes in appetite and weight, unwelcome changes in usual sleep pattern, thoughts of death and suicide. Depression may come on as a relatively sudden and severe problem, it may have crept up on you without you noticing or it may consist of a longer term set of symptoms which are less severe.

It's also common for people who are having a difficult time with an Anxiety disorder to feel depressed as a result of the way Anxiety is interfering with their lives. It's my experience that most patients who experience this will find that their Depression lifts naturally as a result of doing better with Anxiety, and no special treatment for the Depression is necessary. To explain it more simply Anxiety is usually the first state of mind and if the Anxiety is not remedied then Depression can set in.

There are two circumstances under which an Anxiety patient may need specific help for Depression. One is if he or she has become so Depressed in response to Anxiety that they no longer have the energy and motivation to overcome the Anxiety disorder. In this case, either medication or cognitive behavioural methods can be used to help overcome the Depression. The second is the case of a person who experienced a severe Depression before the Anxiety disorder appeared, a Depression which was not just a reaction to the troubles imposed by the Anxiety disorder. This Depression, called a primary depression, is likely to require medication. If you find yourself confused about your symptoms of Anxiety and Depression, and what kind of trouble they may indicate, don't struggle in silence with the confusion.

People with chronic Anxiety disorders may find themselves having lots of thoughts about death, and worry this means they are suicidal, or even homicidal. People with Panic Disorder often have lots of worrisome thoughts about dying, particularly of heart attacks and terrible diseases. People with OCD may have thoughts in which they wonder what stops them from committing some terrible crime, like killing people they love. People with Generalised Anxiety Disorder may have "what if" thoughts in which they worry about becoming so anxious and hopeless that they become suicidal. If you have such thoughts, and find them disturbing, it's a good idea to discuss them with a qualified therapist. People often want to keep these thoughts to themselves, because they feel ashamed of them, and worry that a therapist will over-react and want to hospitalise them. However, these thoughts are a common part of Anxiety disorders, and a therapist who is well versed in the treatment of Anxiety disorders will probably be able to evaluate these thoughts and come to a realistic understanding of what they mean and don't mean. So review these with a therapist, in the same way you would review all the other symptoms you experience.

Depression has been identified as one of the largest public health burdens in the United States and major depressive disorder is considered one of the most common co-occurring disorders in Autism. The co-occurrence of depression in persons with Autism Spectrum Disorders (ASD) can significantly and negatively affect quality of life (Magnuson & Constantino,) 2011. The symptoms of depression may also present differently in individuals with ASD. While the most essential features of major depression in the general population are change in mood and loss of interest, the most common presenting symptoms of depression in individuals with ASD may be significantly increased agitation, self-injury, and temper outbursts (Sovner & Hurley, 1982b4,

Lainhart & Folstein, 1945). Despite these findings, limited research has been conducted on the treatment of depression in ASD, particularly on teens and adults with ASD. There has been no published systematic drug trial for major depressive disorder in persons with ASD and only limited research documenting the concurrence of depressive disorders in these individuals where almost half of adults with Autism will experience depression at some point in their lives.

Depression has been around since biblical times. Though the Bible doesn't use the word "depression" except in a few translations and verses, it's often referenced by other similar words, such as downcast, broken hearted, troubled, miserable, despairing, and mourning among others. Throughout the bible, there are a number of stories about godly, influential men and women of faith, who struggled and battled through dark times of hopelessness and depression. David was troubled and battled deep despair, he writes of his anguish, loneliness, fear of the enemy, his heart-cry over sin, and the guilt he struggled with because of it. We also see his huge grief in the loss of his sons in 2 Samuel. In other places, David's honesty with his own weaknesses gives hope to us who struggle today: "My guilt has overwhelmed me like a burden too heavy to bear." Ps. 38:4.

The great Prophet Elijah was discouraged, weary, and afraid. After great spiritual victories over the prophets of Baal, this mighty man of God feared and ran for his life, far away from the threats of Jezebel. And there in the desert, he sat down and prayed, defeated and worn: "I have had enough Lord, he said. Take my life, I am not better than my ancestors." 1 Kings 19:4

Jonah was angry and wanted to run away. After God called Jonah to go to Nineveh to preach to the people, he fled as far away as could. And after a storm at sea, being swallowed by a giant fish, and then being saved and given a second chance, he obeyed. He preached G-d's message to the people of Nineveh. G-d's mercy reached out to all people who turned to Him. But instead of rejoicing, Jonah got mad: "Now O Lord, take away my life, for it is better for me to die than to live." Jonah 4:3 And even after G-d reached out to Jonah again with great compassion, he responded, "I am angry enough to die." Jonah 4:9

Job suffered through great loss, devastation, and physical illness. This righteous man of G-d lost literally everything. So great was his suffering and tragedy that even his own wife said, "Are you still holding on to your integrity? Curse G-d and die!" Job 2:9. Though Job maintained his faithfulness to G-d throughout his life, he still struggled deeply through the trenches of pain: "Why did I not perish at birth, and die as I came from the womb?" Job 3:11 "I have no peace, no quietness, I have no rest, but only turmoil." Job 3:26. "I loathe my very life, therefore I will give free rein to my complaint and speak out in the bitterness of my soul." Job 10:1 "Terrors overwhelm me... my life ebbs away, days of suffering grip me. Night pierces my bones, my gnawing pains never rest." Job 30:15-17

Moses was grieved over the sin of his people. In his feelings of anger and betrayal from his own people, Moses, as a leader, was about ready to quit. He came down from his mountaintop experience with G-d, commandments in hand, only to find the Israelites in complete chaos and sin. His heart-cry to G-d on their behalf was desperate: "But now, please forgive their sin - but if not, then blot me out of the book you have written." Ex. 32:32

Jeremiah wrestled with great loneliness, feelings of defeat, and insecurity. Also known as the weeping prophet, Jeremiah suffered from constant rejection by the people he loved and reached out to. G-d had called him to preach, yet forbidden him to marry and have children. He lived alone, he ministered alone, he was poor, ridiculed, and rejected by his people. In the midst of it, he displayed great spiritual faith and strength, and yet we also see his honesty as he wrestled with despair and a great sense of failure: "Cursed be the day I was born... why did I ever come out of the womb to see trouble and sorrow and to end my days in shame?" Jer. 20:14,18

So there is evidence that Autism dates as far back as biblical times but did not have an identifying name for these hopeless feelings of despair. Do the Catholics go to confession to un burden themselves and to release the build up of Anxiety that once un burden releases new thoughts and fresh ideas into a troubled mind, through the outpouring of the soul.

It seems that Depression has always been a health problem for human beings. Historical documents written by healers, philosophers, and writers throughout the ages, point to the long-standing existence of depression as a health problem. They also describe the continuous and sometimes very clever struggles people have made to find effective ways to treat this condition. Depression was initially called "melancholia". The earliest accounts of melancholia appeared in ancient Mesopotamian texts in the second millennium B.C. At this time, all mental illnesses were thought to be caused when someone was taken over by demons (possession). They were then treated by priests. A separate class of "physicians" treated physical injuries, but not conditions like depression. The first historical understanding of depression was that depression was a spiritual or mental illness rather than a physical one.

Ancient Greeks and Romans were divided in their thinking about the causes of melancholia. Literature of the time was filled with references to mental illness caused by spirits or demons. In the 400s B.C., the Greek historian Herodotus wrote about a king who was driven mad by evil spirits. The early Babylonian, Chinese, and Egyptian civilisations also viewed mental illness as a form of demonic possession. They used exorcism techniques, such as beatings, restraint, and starvation. These "treatments" were designed to drive demons out of the afflicted person's body. In contrast, early Roman and Greek doctors thought that depression was both a biological and psychological disease. Gymnastics, massage, special diets, music, and baths, as well as a mixture of poppy extract and donkey's milk were used to treat depressive symptoms.

Hippocrates, a Greek physician, suggested that personality traits and mental illnesses were related to balanced or imbalanced body fluids called humours. There were four of these humours: yellow bile, black bile, phlegm and blood. Hippocrates classified mental illnesses into categories that included mania, melancholia (depression), and phrenitis (brain fever). Hippocrates thought that melancholia was caused by too much black bile in the spleen. He used bloodletting (a supposedly therapeutic technique which removed blood from the body), bathing, exercise, and dieting to treat depression. In contrast to Hippocrates' view, the famous Roman philosopher and statesman Cicero argued that melancholia was caused by violent rage, fear and grief. This was a mental explanation for depression rather than a physical one. In the last years before Christ, the influence of Hippocrates faded. The predominant view among educated Romans was that mental illnesses like depression were caused by demons and by the anger of the G-ds.

After the fall of the Roman Empire in the 400s AD, scientific thinking about the causes of mental illness and depression again went backward. During the Middle Ages, religious beliefs, specifically Christianity, dominated popular European explanations of mental illness. Most people thought that mentally ill people were possessed by the devil, demons, or witches. They also thought it was possible for these people to infect others with their madness. Treatments included exorcisms, and other cruller strategies such as drowning and burning. A small minority of doctors continued to believe that mental illness was caused by an imbalanced body, poor diet, and grief. Some people with depression were tied up or locked away in "lunatic asylums". No thought was given at that time to the function of the brain.

The Renaissance began in Italy in the 14th century and spread throughout Europe in the 1500s and 1600s. During this time, thinking about mental illness was characterised again by both forward progress and backward thinking. On the one hand, witch-hunts and executions of the mentally ill were quite common throughout Europe. On the other hand, some doctors returned to the views of Hippocrates, asserting that mental illnesses were due to natural causes, and that witches were actually mentally disturbed people in need of humane medical treatment. In 1621, Robert Burton published Anatomy of Melancholy, in which he described the psychological and social causes of depression. These social causes included issues such as poverty, fear and social isolation. In this work, he recommended diet, exercise, distraction, travel, purgatives (cleansers that purge the body of toxins), bloodletting, herbal remedies, marriage, and even music therapy as treatments for depression. During the beginning of the Age of Enlightenment (the 1700s and early 1800s), it was thought that depression was an inherited, unchangeable weakness of temperament. This led to the common thought that affected people should be shunned or locked up. As a result, most people with mental illnesses became homeless and poor, and some were committed to institutions.

During the late 1700s and early 1800s, there were a variety of complex explanations for depression. Some doctors and authors suggested that aggression was the real cause of depression. They suggested exercise, music, drugs and diet as treatments. They also stressed the importance of discussing problems with a close friend or a doctor. Others thought that depression was caused by an internal conflict between unacceptable impulses and a person's conscience. Advances in general medical knowledge caused other scientists to believe in and search for organic (physical) causes of depression.

In beginning of the 1800s, new therapies for depression were developed. This included water immersion, which involved keeping people under water for as long as possible without drowning them. It also included a special spinning stool to cause dizziness in order to rearrange the contents of the brain into the correct positions. Benjamin Franklin introduced an early form of electroshock therapy. Horseback riding, special diets, enemas, purging and vomiting were also recommended treatments. Depression was first distinguished from schizophrenia in 1895 by the German psychiatrist Emil Kraepelin.

During this same period, psychodynamic theory was invented. Psychoanalysis, the psychotherapy based upon the psychodynamic theory, became increasingly popular as a treatment for depression. In a

71

1917 essay, Sigmund Freud explained melancholia as a response to loss. This was either real loss (such as the death of a spouse), or symbolic loss (such as the failure to achieve an important goal). Freud believed that a person's unconscious anger over loss weakened the ego, which resulted in self-hate and self-destructive behaviour. Freud recommended psychoanalysis (the "talking cure") to resolve unconscious conflicts and reduce the need for self-abusive thoughts and behaviour. Other doctors during this time viewed depression as a physical disease and a brain disorder.

Treatments during the late 1800s and early 1900s were usually not adequate for people with severe depression. Because of the growth of psychiatry and the power of the medical professionals in the 'psy' complex, many desperate people were treated with lobotomy, which is the surgical destruction of the frontal portion of a person's brain. This had become popular as a "calming" treatment at this time. Lobotomies were often unsuccessful. They caused personality changes, inability to make decisions, and poor judgment. Even worse, they sometimes lead to a coma or even death. Electroconvulsive therapy, was a popular treatment for schizophrenia, it was also used sometimes for people with depression but it did not work either.

Influenced by hundreds of years of back and forth debate as to whether depression was best thought of as a mental or physical problem, and by increasing knowledge of the brain and brain chemistry, the medical community of the 1950s and 60's accepted a classification that divided depression into subtypes based on supposed causes of the disorder. "Endogenous" depression came from within the body and was caused by genetics or some other physical problem. People with endogenous depression were supposed to view themselves as the source of their own suffering and accept that there was an internal cause perhaps a chemical one. Their emotional pain was thought to be unaffected by the attitudes or responses of the people around them. In contrast, "neurotic" or "reactive" depression was caused by some significant change in the environment, such as the death of a spouse, or other significant loss, such as the loss of a job. Individuals with reactive depression were thought to feel isolated, victimised and abandoned. They were told to view the cause of their problems as something external to themselves. People with reactive depression were thought to develop bodily symptoms and to make suicide attempts as a means of getting support from the people around them.

The 1950s were also important in the search for organic causes and treatments for mental illness. The practice of using medications to treat mental illness gained greater favour. Psychiatry, which had previously looked to psychotherapy as their therapy of choice, started to emphasize the use of medications as primary treatments for mental illnesses. During the same period, new theories in psychology added to the approaches of psychotherapy. Behaviourism, and the Cognitive Behavioural school of thought, as well as Client - centred (Humanistic) therapy, and Family Systems therapies joined Psychodynamic psychotherapy as popular treatment options.

Currently, rather than adopting either the mind or the body explanation of depression, scientists and mental health professionals recognize that depressive symptoms have multiple causes. In the current view, depression can be caused by both mental and physical causes at the same time. It is no longer necessary to choose a single cause. No single cause is going to be fully explained and account for all types of depression. Because it has become the accepted view that depression frequently has multiple causes, including biological, psychological and social causes, it has also become the normal belief that multiple professions and approaches to treatment have important roles to play in helping people overcome depression.

Later on in Chapter 10 and the visual chart we look at other contributing conditions such as Post Traumatic Stress Disorder (PTSD), Complex PTSD, Complex Trauma and varying feelings of denial. However Science is still slow in linking Depression and Anxiety to the Autistic brain and until such times we are still slow to progress forward other than to find our own solutions and could Autism be the answer to what is causing depression and anxiety in our ancestors descending throughout the ages, including biblical times to the present day because we failing to find solutions to our own problems where our bodies chemicals are linked to the Autistic brain. The good news is whilst depression and anxiety can linger and reoccur some new studies show that it previously was not clear that anyone with depression could recover so fully, so instead of trying to relieve symptoms the goals could be to strive for a deeper sense of fulfilment.

Chapter 5

Spectrum Personality Types

When working with clients and different personality types many clients who come and see me are not aware that they may have an underlying personality condition or disorder. The word disorder can make parts of their personality appear to be quite a negative factor. Many clients feel that there is something amiss but not really quite sure what it is. In the following chapter we are going to look at the different types of personalities and how they could possibly contribute to being on the Autistic Spectrum. People's personality types makes them who they are and very little can be done to change a personality type. People can be controlled by medication or they can change due to external factors that affect them etc: Bereavement or (PTSD) Post Traumatic Stress Disorder, brain damage, or by changing they way they think about certain situations etc. However fundamentally a person's personality type might be genetic with largely pre determined characteristics in the way they see the world, shaped during their earliest years and otherwise affected little by efforts to change.

Many contemporary personality psychologists believe that there are five basic dimensions of personality, often referred to as the "Big 5" personality traits. The five broad personality traits described by the theory are extraversion (also often spelled extroversion), agreeableness, openness, conscientiousness, and neuroticism. The early Greeks believed in the 9 Enneagram of personality types, consisting of the reformer, the helper, the achiever, the individualist, the investigator, the loyalist, the enthusiast, the challenger, and the peacemaker. The Enneagram has identified aspects of Roman Catholicism and Judaism's Kabbalah teaching however theories of personality have long attempted to pin down exactly how many personality traits exist. Later theories have suggested a various number of possible traits, including Gordon Allport's list of 4,000 personality traits, Raymond Cattell's 16 personality factors, and Hans Eysenck's three-factor theory. However, many researchers felt that Cattell's theory was too complicated and Eysenck's was too limited in scope. As a result, the five-factor theory emerged to describe the essential traits that serve as the building blocks of personality. It is important to note that each of the five personality factors represents a range between two extremes. For example, extraversion represents a continuum between extreme extraversion and extreme introversion. In the real world, most people lie somewhere in between the two polar ends of each dimension. Research suggests that both biological and environmental influences play a role in shaping our personalities. These five categories are usually described as follows.

Openness - This trait features characteristics such as imagination and insight. People who are high in this trait also tend to have a broad range of interests. They are curious about the world and other people and eager to learn new things and enjoy new experiences. People who are high in this trait tend to be more adventurous and creative. People low in this trait are often much more traditional and may struggle with abstract thinking.

Conscientiousness - Standard features of this dimension include high levels of thoughtfulness, empathic behaviour, self awareness, good impulse control, and goal-directed behaviours. Highly conscientious people tend to be organised and mindful of details. They plan ahead, think about how their behaviour affects others, and are mindful of deadlines.

Extraversion - Extraversion (or extroversion) is characterised by excitability, sociability, talkativeness, assertiveness, and high amounts of emotional expressiveness. This personality type might have good or poor boundary setting skills for example they may be overly social, overly talkative or overly assertive. Or the exact opposite is introversion (introverted) where they may be reclusive, struggle with sociability and assertiveness skills. People who are high in extraversion are outgoing and tend to gain energy in social situations. Being around other people helps them feel energised and excited. People who are low in extraversion (or introverted) tend to be more reserved and have less energy to expend in social settings. Social events can feel draining and introverts often require a period of solitude and quiet in order to "recharge."

Agreeableness - This personality dimension includes attributes such as trust, altruism, kindness, affection, and other pro social behaviours. People who are high in agreeableness tend to be more cooperative while those low in this trait tend to be more competitive and sometimes even manipulative.

Neuroticism - Neuroticism is a trait characterised by sadness, moodiness, and emotional instability. Individuals who are high in this trait tend to experience mood swings, anxiety, irritability, and sadness. Those low in this trait tend to be more stable and emotionally resilient.

As you can see reading these five key personality dimensions, any one trait or other can generalise and contribute to a personality type, and Autism falls into the broad range of traits of a personality.

Bipolar Disorder for those not familiar with bipolar disorder, is a mood disorder once known as "manic depression." Persons with bipolar disorder alternate between a frenzied state known as mania and episodes of depression. (Bipolar has recently also be classed as schizophrenia with the main characteristic being more hallucinations and paranoid states). While some individuals experience only the manic episodes, many affected individuals rapidly alternate between these two states and experience great irritability. As with other psychiatric disorders, studies suggest that bipolar disorder may be relatively common among children and adults with Autism. Some studies have found that as many as 27 per cent of those with Autism also have symptoms of bipolar disorder. However, I believe that Bipolar disorder is mistakenly over-diagnosed in those with Autism. In part this is because some symptoms can overlap, even though there are currently three distinct types of Bipolar which sub classify the type and duration of manic phases or episodes. Recent research has linked Bi Polar disorder with cycles of the moon, as well as other mood disorders are also affected by the cycles of the moon. During the time that the moon is nearing its "Full Phase", we can notice the escalation in mood changes and the onset of hyperactivity and other impulsive behaviours. For people with Rapid Cycling Bi Polar Disorder which means there moods alter more frequently on a weekly fortnightly basis could be more affected and in tune with the lunar cycles.

The Moon affects everything from tides, to sleep patterns and the behaviour of animals as well as plants. During a New Moon or Full Moon the sap in plants rise, that is why this is the best time to replant something. It makes sense that the cycle of the moon would also affect people. Take into consideration that our bodies are comprised of 65% water and the moon affects the level of the tides while in different phases throughout the month.

The belief that the full moon can excite and disturb human behaviour is deeply rooted in culture, language and clinical lore, but it tends to be regarded as a myth by the scientific community because it is not supported by epidemiological research.

It's particularly challenging to diagnose psychiatric disorders in individuals who have language impairments or intellectual disabilities - as do many persons with Autism. When diagnosing typically developing children and adults, we can ask them about their emotions and experiences. Yet we know that many individuals with Autism have trouble expressing themselves or understanding such questions. Even mild language difficulties can make it difficult to relate thoughts and feelings. For these reasons, traditional methods of assessing psychiatric disorders can be inappropriate for many of those with Autism. It's particularly important for the doctor to get to know the individual and his or her family and environment before attempting such a diagnosis. The challenge is to distinguish symptoms of a mood disturbance from those of Autism or Attention Deficit Hyperactivity Disorder

(ADHD). ADHD is even more commonly associated with Autism. Its symptoms can include extreme frustration and difficulty controlling emotions, as well as hyperactivity, distractibility and impulsivity.

In a study of children with Autism (ages 7 to 17), it was found that nearly a third had frequent episodes of "elevated mood." Just over 60 per cent could be described as "very irritable." Just over half talked excessively. Other common symptoms included excessive activity such as pacing (43 per cent), accident proneness (44 per cent), distractibility (43 per cent) and a tendency to "get in trouble" (47 per cent). Sleep disturbances were also common. The point we are making is here is that all these behaviours could be considered symptoms of Bipolar disorder. Yet it is clear these children did not all have Bipolar disorder. In many cases, their "mania" symptoms were, in fact, symptoms of Autism. ADHD symptoms also overlap with these behaviours which is why it is important for a medical diagnosis.

You can tease apart the symptoms of true Bipolar disorder from those of Autism by looking carefully at when the symptoms appeared and how long they lasted. For example a teenager or adult with Autism who has always been high-energy, happy and socially intrusive shouldn't be labelled as manic just because they talks to strangers and makes inappropriate comments. By contrast, let's say the same teenager or adult abruptly started going without sleep for days in a row, while having more tantrums than usual. This may represent a true manic episode. Therefore the symptoms of Bipolar disorder in someone with Autism are likely to look different than they would in others. They commonly include "pressured speech" (rapid, loud and virtually nonstop talking), constant pacing, an abrupt decrease in sleep and increased impulsivity leading to aggression. Psychiatrists often prescribe psychoactive medications to treat Bipolar disorder. Lithium is one of the most common treatments. Unfortunately, lithium often produces significant side effects. They can include thirst, excessive drinking and bed wetting, shaky hands and even life threatening toxicity. This is of particular concern with individuals who have communication difficulties, as they may not be able to alert caregivers to the side effects they're experiencing. Lithium is also given to many addicts to stop them reacting and craving addictive substances, it helps to calm the high levels of anxiety and with drawl when they are having manic episodes. Does this then underpin that many substance misusers have an undiagnosed Bipolar disorder. It's certainly something that can't be ruled out and needs more scientific research to explore it further. This is only one side to our argument, as many addicts may have one or more than one of many un diagnosed personality disorders or in some instances may have two or three or a combination yet undetermined or diagnosed.

Studies have also suggested that anti-seizure; mood-stabilising medications such as valproic acid may be a safer treatment for those with Autism. We've also seen success with a combination of a mood-stabilising medicine and a low dose of an antipsychotic medication. The atypical antipsychotics risperidone and aripiprazole are both government approved to treat irritability in children with Autism ages 6 and older. It appears that by giving dosages of a small amount of an approved drug medication daily, seem to balance out some severe or problematic autism behaviours. Does this create further problems of dependency or raise issues when they withdraw? Some children as they have got older are able to fully stop taking the prescribed medication, and the behaviours are reduced, others are on it for life creating a prescribed dependency.

For adults who have no diagnosis and have turned to self medication, on street drugs, they are un aware of the reasons why they may have become addicted in the first place could it be because they may have undiagnosed Autism?

My best example of this is to imagine splitting a brain in half, the right side of the brain is spinning in an anti clock wise direction and spinning at such a speed its raising slightly up, away from the level of the other side of the brain on the left. We could simply say that one part of the brain is 'out of synch' acting in a problematic way. Without medication the right side of the brain will continue to act in this manner, the impact that this will have will affect thought process, mobility and behaviour, mood swings is sometimes a lot faster, it can also produce negative and intrusive patterns to normalised behavioural characteristics. When the brain (amygdala) is properly medicated with the right balance of chemicals the right side of the brain will calm down and the left side of the brain will be able to slot and fit in together with the right side of the over active brain, forming a complete unit of balance and calmness. Could it be in an over generalisation that people could be turning to alternative street medication to quell the brains activity because they are missing the chemicals needed to quieten the brain. Sometimes some surface reactions to this active side of the brain can form in the way of anxiety behaviours. If the anxiety is left untreated or treated inconsistently with street medication longer term depression can set in.

In addition to medication, researchers are evaluating a family treatment intervention that combines education and psychotherapy to help individuals with Autism and mood disorders. Early results suggest that this type of intervention decreases mood severity in children, while improving family interactions and access to appropriate healthcare. Maturation may have an impact on the five dimensions. As people age, they tend to become less extraverted, less neurotic, and less open to experience. Agreeableness and conscientiousness, on the other hand, tend to increase as people grow older.   It is always important to remember that behaviour involves an interaction between a person's underlying personality and situational variables. Bi Polar is not curable but with help to manage it with mood stabilisers the situation that a person finds himself or herself in plays a major role in how the person reacts. However, in most cases, people offer responses that are consistent with their underlying personality traits. These dimensions represent broad areas of personality. These groupings of characteristics tend to occur together in many people. For example, individuals who are sociable tend to be talkative. However, these traits do not always occur together. Personality is complex and varied and each person may display behaviours across several of these dimensions.

Bipolar and Borderline personality disorder and often the two can be confused easily as they both sound similar, and Borderline Personality Disorder can be abbreviated (BPD) which adds to the confusion even further. There is a differentiating factor between them, Symptoms of Borderline Personality disorder are pretty consistent and on going, while people with Bipolar disorder appear to have 'breaks' between their extreme mood swings; the extreme ups and downs that sufferers of both disorders must deal with can make them look awfully similar from the outside. However those with Borderline personality feel a disconnected empty sense of self; have problems regulating emotions and may be quite detached from who they actually are, which is detrimental to relationships.

Those with Borderline Personality have several of the following characteristics they don't accept responsibility for their actions and will actually accuse someone else of any wrongdoing that is their own. They don't remember situations the way everyone else does. They will replace negative reflexive memories with memories that make others the "evil" ones. They claim to not remember anything at all. They do not engage in communication in an adult fashion. They project their own faults, shortcomings, negativity, poor self esteem, and other issues onto others, including their own children. They can be physically violent, but more often are very hostile and aggressive when cornered or called out because of their behaviour, they cannot see their own faults or reasons why their behaviour might be to blame because of the disconnected sense of self. In extreme cases, they will play a very unpleasant and malicious "blame game" that causes extensive emotional and psychological hurt to someone one else, but then tell that person "it's for your own good" or "it's your fault this is happening". Those are some of the extreme behaviours where there is a complete lack of self awareness and emotions.

Some people with Borderline personality may feel emotions incredibly strongly and feel compassion deeply, but in our experience this is not in every situation. This is where an overlap may occur with Autistic Spectrum Conditions or even with other personality disorders. Whilst one person may have the experience of a strong negative Borderline consistent personality, traits of their Autism personality may kick in and they may be completely compassionate to a wounded animal they accidently came across but lack an emotional regard to a human being. So it's difficult to determine as there is no continuous black and white personality there are lots of shades of grey in between. Other positive traits of BPD can include: loyalty, creativity, empathetic, relentlessness, and adaptability. Individuals with Borderline Personality Disorder may display impulsivity in at least two areas that are potentially self-damaging. They may gamble, spend money irresponsibly, binge eat, abuse substances, engage in unsafe sex, or drive recklessly. There may be an identity disturbance characterised by markedly and persistently unstable self-image or sense of self. There may be sudden and dramatic shifts in self-image, characterised by shifting goals, values, and vocational aspirations. There may be sudden changes in opinions and plans about career, sexual identity, values, and types of friends. Individuals may suddenly change from the role of a needy supplicant for help to a righteous avenger of past mistreatment. Individuals with Borderline Personality Disorder may also sometimes display recurrent suicidal behaviour, gestures, or threats, or self-mutilating behaviours. Completed suicide occurs in 8%-10% of such individuals, and self-mutilation acts (e.g., cutting or burning) and suicide threats and attempts are very common. Recurrent suicidality is often the reason that these individuals present for help. These self-destructive acts are usually precipitated by threats of separation or rejection or by expectations that they assume increased responsibility. Self-mutilation may occur during dissociative experiences and often brings relief by reaffirming the ability to feel or by expiating the individual's sense of self. Borderline individuals do not respect themselves which is why suicidal ideation's occur for the attention the release of self harm does, borderline individuals use self harm as a coping mechanism usually to release past pain. Some don't understand fully why they do it as there can be a lack of self awareness or context blindness in this area.

Individuals with Borderline Personality Disorder may display affective instability that is due to a marked reactivity of mood (e.g., intense episodic dysphoria, irritability, or anxiety usually lasting a few hours and only rarely more than a few days). The basic dysphoric mood of those with Borderline Personality Disorder is often disrupted by periods of anger, panic, or despair and is rarely relieved by periods of well-being or satisfaction. These episodes may reflect the individual's extreme reactivity to interpersonal stresses.

Individuals with Borderline Personality Disorder may be troubled by chronic feelings of emptiness. Easily bored, they may constantly seek something to do. Individuals with Borderline Personality Disorder frequently express inappropriate, intense anger or have difficulty controlling their anger. They may display extreme sarcasm, enduring bitterness, or verbal outbursts. The anger is often elicited when a caregiver or lover is seen as neglectful, withholding, uncaring, or abandoning. Such expressions of anger are often followed by shame and guilt and contribute to the feeling they have.

On the other hand the core personality trait of an Empath is the ability to experience the emotions of others as if they were their own emotions. For the untrained Empath, this can be overpowering at times. They often feel emotionally exhausted due to the sheer amount of emotion thrust upon them. Empaths are uniquely placed to understand the thoughts and motivations of others, so they have a keen sense of fairness and justice as they know that we all experience the same kinds of feelings and emotions. Seeing injustice in the world gets to an Empath way more than it would a normal person. Some people might accuse an Empath of being overly invested in this way, but it is more like the Empath is immune to being desensitised to injustice and inequality. Empaths are highly attuned to other people's moods, good and bad. They feel everything, sometimes to an extreme. They take on negativity such as anger or anxiety, which can be exhausting for them. If they are around peace and love, though, their bodies take these on and flourish. Many empaths are introverted.

Empaths become overwhelmed in crowds, which can amplify their empathy. They tend to be introverted and prefer one-to-one contact or small groups. Even if an empath is more extraverted they may prefer to limit how much time they spend in a crowd or at a party. Empaths are highly intuitive Empaths experience the world through their intuition. It is important for them to develop their intuition and listen to their gut feelings about people. This helps empaths find positive relationships and avoid energy draining vampires. Empaths need alone time as super-responders, empaths find being around people can be draining, so they periodically need time alone to recharge. Even a brief escape prevents emotional overload. For example, empaths like to take their own cars when they go places so they can leave when they please. Empaths are also highly spiritually in tune and are often clairvoyants. Empaths can become overwhelmed in intimate relationships; too much togetherness can be difficult for an Empath so they may avoid intimate relationships. Deep down they are afraid of being engulfed and losing their identity. For Empaths to be at ease in a relationship, the traditional paradigm for being a couple must be redefined.

But how could someone on the Autism Spectrum feel emotion especially as Autistics are supposed to have alexithymia (inability to read faces, recognise emotion or verbalise emotion). Current science presumes that stereotypical autism is alexitymic but as an Empath and fellow autistic I have an ability to read emotion, people's faces, body language and a person's personality, which indicates to me that I am on the opposite end of the spectrum. Some autistic empaths are able to recognise faces and names of thousands of people, where there is no face blindness or may appear to have a photographic memory for places, pictures and objects. Some pro gamblers are able to read people in a hand of poker by facial gestures and body language. So depending on where you sit on the emotional scale is all an indicator of your Emotional Intelligence (EI) and as we discover more about our emotions further research is coming to the forefront.

Empathy is the ability to feel along with others. Sympathy is the ability to feel for others. People with autism spectrum disorder may appear to be both un empathetic and unsympathetic. They may laugh when someone is injured, or respond with little or no emotion to another person's grief or joy. Scientists have yet to discover the level and intensity of sensitivity of the spectrum and the people within it and as more questions are raised about the empathy levels of autistics the current climate is rather divided scientists categorically cannot state that it is impossible for any autistic spectrum individual to experience high levels of empathy.

However as Emotional intelligence is almost the opposite of emotional empathy. It is an ability to manage and control your emotions, those with emotional intelligence are able to identify not just their emotions but those of others as well. Emotional intelligence is said to be made up of three key abilities: Identifying one's own and others' emotions being able to harness these emotions and use them to solve problems, and the ability to control one's own, and other's emotions. Experts have recognised that emotional intelligence is an important leadership skill. People who possess it typically have other good leadership abilities as well. They are self-aware, motivated, are good at self-regulating and have above-average social skills and they can also have empathy.

Psychopathic personality disorders also raise questions about emotional empathy. But are the two connected when it comes to psychopathy? Psychopaths are noted for their lack of empathy. In fact, a deficit of emotion appears to be a prerequisite for psychopathy. There are studies that have shown psychopaths are unable to respond normally to emotionally-charged words or pictures. They also have trouble recognising emotional faces. So does this mean that because they do not feel emotion themselves, they cannot recognise emotions in others? Well, they might not be able to recognise it, but they can certainly use it to their advantage. Psychopaths are renowned for using superficial charm and manipulation to get what they want from others. This means they are highly skilled at reading people's emotions. Therefore, by inference, they have to have some degree of emotional intelligence. Psychopaths use their emotional intelligence as a form of manipulation. This is to inflict the greatest amount of harm to their victims.

They will be able to identify a person's weakness or vulnerabilities and attack without remorse.

There is a link between them but let's first clarify about primary and secondary psychopaths. Characteristics of Primary Psychopaths include Aggression, Dominance, Organised, Grandiose, Fearless, Extrovert, Lack of Emotion and No Anxiety. Characteristics of secondary Psychopaths include Impulsive, Unorganised, Risk-taking, Reactive aggression, Normal to high levels of anxiety, Prone to boredom, and insular with depression that could lead to suicide. There have been numerous studies supporting the notion that psychopaths have reduced emotional responses when viewing disturbing or upsetting material. However we have found no study that examined how the emotional intelligence differs between the primary and secondary psychopaths and some psychopaths are able to control some of their bodily responses to emotional stimuli in order to manipulate others and benefit themselves.

Early theories suggested that all psychopaths were highly intelligent. However, this didn't take into account the primary and secondary types or emotional intelligence. Typical psychopaths portrayed in Hollywood blockbusters, individuals such as Hannibal Lecter tend to be primary psychopaths. He is a lone predator who is cunning and manipulative. They are also all likely to have high emotional intelligence and low emotional empathy. Then there is the less commonly portrayed secondary psychopath. The one who is impulsive, takes risks and is easily bored. You could count Iron Man- Tony Stark as such an individual. He has all these secondary psychopathic traits. These types are likely to have low emotional intelligence but high emotional empathy.

The vast majority of persons with Autism Spectrum Disorders are highly moral but can show aggression of a non-lethal severity. Nevertheless there are a small number of persons with Autism who do show lethal violence. The rate of these problems in special hospitals and prisons is almost twice the general population prevalence of Autism.

Originally, these conditions were called Autistic Psychopathy by Hans Asperger 1938 and 1944. We are suggesting that we bring back the diagnosis of Autistic Psychopathy for those persons with Autism who engage in criminal activities with the new diagnosis Criminal Autistic Psychopathy. These persons have the dual features of Autism and Psychopathy. The seriousness of this condition is often missed with the sole diagnosis of Autism and generally they may have an anti social personality or conduct disorder, there are overlapping features but also differences from General Psychopathy. Many of the personality traits are similar but can appear more extreme.

Sociopathic behaviours we would describe as being a lesser form of psychopathy without the severe criminal behaviour attached to it, but a large number of the characteristics are similar. Psychologists vie to enumerate the facets of sociopathic behaviours. The sociopath has an attention bottleneck that allows him to focus only on one activity or train of thought, to the exclusion of others. Researchers, say that the sociopath lacks not "moral" identity but self-identity altogether. In The Mask of Sanity, published in 1941, Cleckley distilled what he believed to be the 16 key behavioural characteristics that defined psychopathy. Most of these factors are still used today to diagnose sociopaths/psychopaths and others with antisocial disorders. (Psychopathy and Sociopathic terms are together intertwined in clinical history, and they are now largely used interchangeably. The DSM excludes both in favour of antisocial personality disorder.) the 16 characteristics are: Superficial charm and good intelligence, absence of delusions and other signs of irrational thinking, absence of nervousness or neurotic manifestations, unreliability, untruthfulness and insincerity, lack of remorse and shame, Inadequately motivated antisocial behaviour, poor judgment and failure to learn by experience, pathologic egocentricity and incapacity for love, general poverty in major affective reactions, specific loss of insight, unresponsiveness in general interpersonal relations, and failure to follow any life plan.

A sociopath is a term used to describe someone who has antisocial personality disorder (ASPD). People with ASPD can't understand others' feelings. They'll often break rules or make impulsive decisions without feeling guilty for the harm they cause. People with ASPD may also use "mind games" to control friends, family members, co-workers, and even strangers. They may also be perceived as charismatic or charming.

However Narcissistic personality disorder involves a distorted self-image. Emotions can be unstable and intense, and there is excessive concern with vanity, prestige, power, and personal adequacy (often strongly linked to histrionic personality over dramatisation). There also tends to be a lack of empathy and an exaggerated sense of superiority. Narcissistic personality disorder (NPD) is closely associated with egocentrism, a personality characteristic in which people see themselves and their interests and opinions as the only ones that really matter. People with NPD have limited interest in the feelings of others. They lack empathy and are unable to feel or appreciate feelings that are not their own. A person with NPD has an excessive sense of self-importance, an intense preoccupation with themselves, and a lack of empathy for others. Narcissistic personality disorder (NPD) is characterised by an extreme sense of self-worth. The term comes from a character in Greek mythology, called Narcissus. He saw his reflection in a pool of water and fell in love with it. NPD is one of a group of conditions known as dramatic personality disorders. The person will have unstable and intense emotions and a distorted self image. An unusual love of self, an excessive sense of importance and superiority, and a preoccupation with success and power can indicate a lack of self-confidence. NPD often involves a deep sense of insecurity and a lack of self esteem.

It is noticeable that people with NPD, do not show a major degree of functioning problems in stress free environment or when they are supported (except that they are perceived as "not pleasant characters" to deal with). However under stress and without support they can become quite dysfunctional in a way not far from what we usually see in other autism-like behaviours. Another perspective that suggests similarities between narcissism and autistic spectrum disorders involves

Theory of Mind. "One of the key traits in people with autism is that they lack what is known in psychology as a 'theory of mind', which is also known as 'mind blindness'. Theory of mind (T.O.M) means the ability to understand that other people have a mind and thoughts that differ from our own. This means that people with autism will often only be able to see things from their own point of view, they cannot imagine how something may affect someone else; which may be why you see them as self-centred." People who are narcissistic experience difficulties when differences arise between themselves and others because of this deficit in "theory of mind." It is hard for them to believe that there is another side to the issue that troubles them because they believe that their view is the only view, that they are always "right," and that listening to the other's feelings either makes them at fault or may block their ability to get what they want. If they don't get what they want or if they are harmed in the process narcissistic rage is one of the most aggressive forms of rage which is where their ego has been attacked and they will drop you as if you never existed.

If narcissistic personality disorder tendencies stem from neuro-biological deficits and/or brain anomalies that cause difficulties with empathy, then it becomes easier to empathise with rather than become angry at an emotionally-deaf loved one. However NPD can and has become the root of many faulty relationships and domestic abuse where the NP supersedes that of the empath where the balance of the relationship no longer is 50/50. Science suggests NPD is developed at a young age from when a child is unable to get their needs met. I believe as with all these personalities it is genetic and you were more than likely to have an ancestor with the same condition. I look forward to reading what neuroscience research finds in the way of biological clues as to why narcissism and Autism seem linked.

What is schizoid personality disorder. Schizoid personality disorder is a type of eccentric personality disorder. A person with this disorder behaves differently from most other people. This may include avoiding social interactions, or seeming to be aloof or lacking personality. However, people with this disorder are able to function fairly well in society. This condition is usually diagnosed in early adulthood. Symptoms include: being detached, preferring to be alone, avoiding social situations not desiring relationships, seeming dull or indifferent, inability to enjoy activities trouble relating to others, lacking motivation. Most people with this condition have a relative with schizophrenia, schizoid personality disorder, or schizotypal personality disorder. Other risk factors include: environmental factors, which seem to have the most impact during childhood, experiencing abuse or neglect as a child or having an emotionally detached parent. The term schizoid can be used when a personality is split for example either viewing oneself as all good or all bad, the all good alternates with the all bad, and we can struggle as to how we see oneself. Both views are equally unrealistic and usually can date back to early childhood experiences and reflect back to how the child felt when interacting with the primary caregiver. They also reflect the irreconcilable nature of the child's experience with the caregiver who generally treated them in this split in a very unnuanced way.

SPD is not the same as schizophrenia or schizotypal personality disorder, but there is some evidence of links and shared genetic risk between SPD, other cluster A personality disorders, and schizophrenia. Thus, SPD is considered to be a "schizophrenia-like personality disorder. Very little research has been done in this area, but SPD can also go into a fantasy related type of behaviour, so when an outcome is failed to be reached by the brain and anxiety sets in schizoid behaviour goes into fantasy mode as in the term paranoid schizoid position where the brains way of finding a an answer of solution is to find ones from its own memories. A pathological reliance on fantasising and preoccupation with inner experience is often part of the schizoid withdrawal from the world. Fantasy thus becomes a core component of the self in exile, though fantasising in schizoid individuals is far more complicated than a means of facilitating withdrawal, this can be also known as splitting, so when something is all good and we don't want all good any more we want bad, we split our mind automatically and can revert to self sabotaging behaviour.

Paranoid refers to the central paranoid anxiety, the fear of invasive malevolence. This is experienced as coming from the outside, but ultimately derives from the projection out of the death instinct. Paranoid anxiety can be understood in terms of anxiety about imminent annihilation and derives from a sense of the destructive or death instinct of the child. In this position before the secure internalisation of a good object to protect the ego, the immature ego deals with its anxiety by splitting off bad feelings and projecting them out. However, this causes paranoia. Schizoid refers to the central defence mechanism: splitting, the vigilant separation of the good object from the bad object.

Theorist Melanie Klein posited that healthy development requires that an infant split its external world, its objects and itself into two categories: good (i.e., gratifying, loved, loving) and bad (i.e. frustrating, hated, persecutory). This splitting makes it possible to introject and identify with the good. In other words: splitting in this stage is useful because it protects the good from being destroyed by the bad. Later, when the ego has developed sufficiently, the bad can be integrated, and ambivalence and conflict can be tolerated. In relation to most of the personality conditions discussed in this chapter, you may realise one or more of your relatives may have the same or one of these types of personalities. People who have SPD may also suffer from clinical depression. However, this is not always the case. Unlike depressed people, persons with SPD generally do not consider themselves inferior to others. They may recognize that they are "different." However Schizoid and narcissistic personality disorders can seem similar in some respects (e.g. both show identity confusion, may lack warmth and spontaneity, avoid deep relationships with intimacy). Another commonality observed is intellectual hypertrophy which leads to a lack of rootedness in bodily existence. There are, nonetheless, important differences. The schizoid hides his need for dependency and is rather fatalistic, passive, cynical, overtly bland or vaguely mysterious. The narcissist is, in contrast, ambitious and competitive and exploits others for his dependency needs. There are also parallels between SPD and obsessive-compulsive personality disorder (OCPD), such as detachment, restricted emotional expression and rigidity. However, in

OCPD the capacity to develop intimate relationships is usually intact but deep contacts may be avoided because of an unease with emotions and a devotion to work.

In autism there may be substantial difficulty in distinguishing, sometimes called "Schizoid disorder of childhood," from SPD. In the USA Autism used to be referred to as Schizophrenia of childhood or childhood psychosis which was rejected in the UK. (The USA has tended to use the schizophrenia more widely than in the UK)

But while AS is an autism-spectrum disorder, SPD is classified as a "schizophrenia-like" personality disorder. There is some overlap as some people with autism also qualify for a diagnosis of schizotypal or schizoid PD. However, one of the distinguishing features of schizoid PD is a restricted affect and an impaired capacity for emotional experience and expression. Persons with AS are "hypo-mentalizers", i.e., they fail to recognize social cues such as verbal hints, body language and gesticulation, but those with schizophrenia- like personality disorders tend to be "hyper-mentalizers," overinterpreting such cues in a generally suspicious way (see imprinted brain theory). Although they may have been socially isolated from childhood onward, most people with schizoid personality disorder displayed well-adapted social behaviour as children, along with apparently normal emotional function. SPD does also not involve impairments in nonverbal communication such as a lack of eye contact, unusual prosody or a pattern of restricted interests or repetitive behaviours. Compared to AS, SPD is characterised by prominent conduct disorder, better adult adjustment, less severely impaired social interaction and a slightly increased risk of schizophrenia.

Dependent personality disorder (DPD) is a personality disorder that is characterised by a pervasive psychological dependence on other people. This personality disorder is a long-term condition in which people depend on others to meet their emotional and physical needs, with only a minority achieving normal levels of independence. Dependent personality disorder is a Cluster C personality disorder, characterised by excessive fear and anxiety. It begins by early adulthood, and it is present in a variety of contexts and is associated with inadequate functioning. Symptoms can include anything from extreme passivity, devastation or helplessness when relationships end, avoidance of responsibilities and severe submission.

There is a considerable overlap in symptoms between Austism and certain personality disorders. Similarities and differences of the concepts are discussed in the framework of the Diagnostic and Statistical Manual of Mental Disorders, but as yet no clear definition or extensive research provides us with answers so through our own intellect we are still searching for the answers and hopefully in the next few chapters we may find them.

Chapter 6

Sexuality and Gender

Gender and where does this fit in on the Spectrum? Many people when we first started talking about gender being on the Autism Spectrum thought we should not start talking about a subject that was fraught with controversy. We would like to say that we are not opposed to anyone's gender, we are drawing upon theories that might explain why people feel the way that they do and answer unanswered questions people feel inside. If you are comfortable with your gender that's fine, we are not criticising or defining one gender over another, we do believe that the whole gender subject should have a distinct section on the Autistic Spectrum which it has never had before. Years ago transgender rights were barely heard of, now the subject has become of the most toxic incendiary issues of our age so please do not throw us all to the wolves as we are trying to help find the answers too.

There is an on going list of gender identities. If you see an identity with a confusing or wrong description, please feel free to contact us about it and we will answer as soon as possible. Feel free to mix and match your own prefixes and suffixes to create the identity that best describes you. At present the list we have derived from the internet alphabetically includes:

List of Genders

Abimegender:	profound, deep,infinite; resembles when one mirror is reflecting into another mirror creating an infinite paradox
Adamasgender:	Refuses to be categorized.

Androgyne:	Middle of the gender spectrum between male and female.
Aerogender:	Influenced by your surroundings.
Aesthetigender:	derived from an aesthetic; also known as videgender,
Affectugender:	Affected by mood swings.
Agender:	Feeling of no gender/absence of gender or neutral gender.
Agenderflux:	Fluctuating feelings of masculinity of femininity, but NOT male or female.
Alexigender:	fluid between more than one gender but the individual cannot tell what those genders
Aliusgender:	removed from common gender descriptors and guidelines
Amaregender:	A gender that changes depending on who you're in love with.
Ambigender:	feeling of two genders simultaneously without fluctuation; ambidextrous, only
Ambonec:	identifying as both man and woman, yet neither at the same time Amicagender: a gender that changes depending on which friend you're with
Androgyne:	Sometimes used in the case of "androgynous presentation"; describes the feeling of being a mix of both masculine and feminine (and sometimes neutral) gender qualities.
Anesigender:	Feeling like a certain gender yet comfortable identifying with another.
Angenital:	a desire to be without primary sexual characteristics, without necessarily being genderless; one may be both

Angenital:	And identify as any other gender alongside.
Anogender:	A gender that fades in and out but always comes back to the same feeling.
Anongender:	A gender that is unknown to both yourself and others.
Antegender:	A protean gender which has the potential to be anything, but is formless and motionless, and therefore, does not manifest as any particular gender.
Anxiegender:	A gender that is affected by anxiety.
Apagender:	a feeling of apathy towards ones gender which leads to them not looking any further
Apconsugender:	You know what it isn't, but not what it is; the gender is hiding itself from you.
Astergender:	A gender that feels bright and celestial.
Astralgender:	a gender that feels connected to space
Autigender:	A gender only be understood in the context of being autistic. Meant for autistic people
Autogender:	A gender experience that is deeply personal to oneself.
Axigender:	two genders that sit on opposite ends of an axis; one being a gender and the other being any other gender; these genders are experienced one at a time with no overlapping and with very short transition time.
Bigender:	the feeling of having two genders either at the same time or separately; usually used to describe feeling "traditionally male" and "traditionally female", but does not have to
Biogender	A gender that feels connected to nature in some way.

Blurgender:	More than one gender that blur together not being able to distinguish or identify individual genders; synonymous with genderfuzz.
Boyflux:	Mostly or all male most of the time but experience fluctuating intensity of male identity.
Burstgender:	gender that comes in intense bursts of feeling and quickly fades back to the original
Caelgender:	qualities with outer space or has the aesthetic of space, stars, nebulas, etc.
Cassgender:	The feeling of gender is unimportant to you.
Cassflux:	When the level of indifference towards your gender fluctuates.
Cavusgender:	For people with depression; one gender when not depressed and another when.
Cendgender:	When your gender changes between one and its opposite.
Ceterofluid:	Your feelings fluctuate between masculine, feminine, and neutral.
Ceterogender:	A nonbinary gender with specific masculine, feminine, or neutral feelings.
Cisgender:	The gender you were assigned at birth, all the time (assigned (fe)male/feeling (fe)male).
Cloudgender:	A gender that cannot be fully realized or seen clearly due to depersonalization/ derealization disorder.
Collgender:	Having too many genders simultaneously to describe each one.

Colorgender:	associated with one or more colours and the feelings, hues, emotions, and/or objects associated with that colour; may be used like pinkgender, bluegender, yellowgender
Commogender:	When you know you aren't cisgender, but you settled with your assigned gender.
Condigender:	A gender that is only felt during certain circumstances.
Deliciagender:	From the Latin word delicia meaning "favorite", meaning the feeling of having more than one simultaneous gender yet preferring one that fits better.
Demifluid:	the feeling your gender being fluid throughout all the demigenders; the feeling of having multiple genders, some static and some fluid
Demiflux:	the feeling of having multiple genders, some static and some fluctuating
Demigender:	A gender that is partially one gender and partially another.
Domgender:	Having more than one gender yet one being more dominant than the others.
Demi-vapor (term coined by @cotton-blossom-jellyfish):	Continuously drifting to other genders, feeling spiritually transcendental when doing so while having a clear - slightly blurred- inner visual of your genders, transitions, and positive emotions.
Tied to Demi-Smoke. Demi-smoke (term coined by @cotton-blossom-jellyfish):	A transcendental, spiritual gender roughly drifting to other genders that are unable to be foreseen and understood, shrouded in darkness within your inner visual. Elevating through mystery. Caused by a lack of inner interpretation and dark emotional states.

Demigirl:	Identifying as partly female and partly male or another gender.
Demiboy:	Identifying as partly male and partly female or another gender.
Duragender:	from the Latin word dura meaning "long-lasting", meaning a subcategory of multigender in which one gender is more identifiable, long lasting, and prominent than the other genders.
Egogender:	So personal to your experience that it can only be described as "you". Epicene: sometimes used synonymously with the adjective "androgynous"; the feeling either having or not displaying characteristics of both or either binary gender; sometimes used to describe feminine male identifying individuals.
Espigender:	Is related to being a spirit or exists on a higher or extra dimensional plane.
Exgender:	The outright refusal to accept or identify in, on, or around the gender spectrum.
Existigender:	A gender that only exists or feels present when thought about or when a conscious effort is made to notice it. Female: one of two binary genders where one feels fully and completely female; can and is used in conjunction with other gender labels and identities.
Femfluid:	Fluctuating or fluid gender feelings that are limited to feminine genders.
Femgender:	A nonbinary gender which is feminine in nature.

Fluidflux:	Fluid between two or more genders that also fluctuate in intensity; a combination of genderfluid and genderflux.
Gemigender:	Having two opposite genders that work together, being fluid and flux together.
Genderblank:	A gender that can only be described as a blank space; when gender is called into question, all that comes to mind is a blank space.
Genderflow:	Fluid between infinite feelings.
Genderfluid:	Fluidity within your gender identity; feeling a different gender as time passes or as situations change; not restricted to any number of genders.
Genderflux:	Your gender fluctuating in intensity; like genderfluid but between one gender and agender.
Genderfuzz:	Coined by lolzmelmel; the feeling of having more than one gender that are somehow blurred together to the point of not being able to distinguish or identify individual genders; synonymous with blurgender.
Gender Neutral:	Having a neutral gender, whether somewhere in between masculine and feminine or a third gender that is separate from the binary; often paired with neutrois.
Genderpunk:	A gender identity that actively resists gender norms.
Genderqueer:	originally used as an umbrella term for nonbinary individuals; may be used as an identity; describes a nonbinary gender regardless of whether the individual is masculine or feminine leaning.

Genderwitched:	A gender in which one is intrigued or entranced by the idea of a particular gender, but is not certain that they are actually feeling it.
Girlflux:	When one feels mostly or all female most of the time but experiences fluctuating intensities of female identity.
Glassgender:	A gender that is very sensitive and fragile.
Glimragender:	A faintly shining, wavering gender.
Greygender:	having a gender that is mostly outside of the binary but is weak and can barely be felt
Gyragender:	Having multiple genders but understanding none of them.
Healgender:	A gender that once realised, brings lots of peace, clarity, security, and creativity to the individual's mind.
Heliogender:	a gender that is warm and burning
Hemigender:	A gender that is half one gender and half something else; one or both halves may be identifiable genders.
Horogender:	A gender that changes over time with the core feeling remaining the same.
Hydrogender:	A gender which shares qualities with water.
Imperigender:	A fluid gender that can be controlled by the individual.
Intergender:	The feeling of gender falling somewhere on the spectrum between masculine and feminine. Meant for intersex people only.
Juxera:	A feminine gender similar to girl, but on a separate plane and off to itself.

Libragender:	A gender that feels agender but has a strong connection to another gender. Male: one of two binary genders where one feels fully and completely male; can and is used in conjunction with other gender labels and identities.
Magigender:	A gender that is mostly gender and the rest is something else.
Mascfluid:	A gender that is fluid in nature, and restricted only to masculine genders.
Mascgender:	A non-binary gender which is masculine in nature.
Maverique:	Taken from the word maverick; the feeling of having a gender that is separate from masculinity, femininity, and neutrality, but is not agender; a form of third gender.
Mirrorgender:	A gender that changes to fit the people around you.
Molligender:	a gender that is soft, subtle, and subdued
Multigender:	The feeling of having more than one simultaneous or fluctuating gender; simultaneous with multigenderand omnigender.
Nanogender:	Feeling a small part of one gender with the rest being something else.
Neutrois:	Having a neutral gender; sometimes a lack of gender that leads to feeling neutral.
Nonbinary:	originally an umbrella term for any gender outside the binary of cisgenders; may be used as an individual identity; occasionally used alongside of genderqueer, the gender identity is neither exclusively female nor exclusively male.

Omnigender:	the feeling of having more than one simultaneous or fluctuating gender; simultaneous with multigenderand polygender.
Oneirogender:	coined by anonymous, "being agender, but having recurring fantasies or daydreams of being a certain gender without the dysphoria or desire to actually be that gender day-to-day".
Pangender:	the feeling of having every gender; this is considered problematic by some communities and thus has been used as the concept of relating in some way to all genders as opposed to containing every gender identity; only applies to genders within one's own culture.
Paragender:	the feeling very near one gender and partially something else which keeps you from feeling fully that gender.
Perigender:	identifying with a gender but not as a gender.
Polygender:	the feeling of having more than one simultaneous or fluctuating gender; simultaneous with multigender and omnigender often used to describe having more than 4 genders..
Proxvir:	a masculine gender similar to boy, but on a separate plane and off to itself.
Quoigender:	feeling as if the concept of gender is inapplicable or nonsensical to one's self
Subgender:	mostly agender with a bit of another gender.

Surgender:	having a gender that is 100% one gender but with more of another gender added on top of that.
Systemgender:	a gender that is the sum of all the genders within a multiple or median system. Transgender: a gender that stretches over the whole spectrum of genders. Transgender: any gender identity that transcends or does not align with your assigned gender or society's idea of gender; the feeling of being any gender that does not match your assigned gender.
Transneutral:	A term used to describe transgender people who were assigned male or female at birth, but identify with neutral gendered feelings to a greater extent than with femininity or masculinity. It is used the same way as "transfeminine" or "transmasculine", but for neutral feelings. It can be used to describe gendered feelings, or as a gender itself..
Trigender:	the feeling of having three simultaneous or fluctuating genders.
Transexual:	happy for others to know you are having medical treatment to change sex.
Transman:	Born female but now identifies as a man.
Transwoman:	Born male but now identifies as a woman.
Transfeminine:	Born male but identifying with a feminine gender. Two Spirit: From native American cultures a person who has both masculine and feminine spirits. Third Gender: Someone categorised by themselves or society as neither male or female..

Vapogender:	feels like smoke; on a shallow level but once you go deeper, it disappears and you are left with no gender and only tiny wisps of what you thought it was.
Venngender:	when two genders overlap creating an entirely new gender; like a venn diagram.
Verangender:	a gender that seems to shift/change the moment it is identified.
Vibragender:	a gender that is usually one stable gender but will occasionally changes or fluctuate before stabilising again.
Vocigender:	a gender that is weaker form of gender. (Many of the genders specified are repeated but with different names).

We as humans have a number of 'male' and 'female' hormones. As Autistics the level and greatness in intensity varies from individual to individual. Most people describe themselves as heterosexual, that means their sexual choice of partner is the opposite sex to themselves. Some women can carry more male hormones than female hormones that make up a females strength of character, behaviours, traits and so on. On the other hand men may carry more female hormones than women and can show sensitivities that some women may not. Questionably you could argue that environmentally there have been significant changes as men are now developing larger breasts and in some cases bigger than women. Is this due to the environment and the foods that we eat the pesticides that are in the food, the fact that more women are taking hormone pills to stop pregnancy and are urinating it away which ends up by precipitation in the atmosphere, in the sea. The rain water in rivers is what the animals drink which intern keeps the cycle going around and around.

Or is it more fundamental than that, where gender differences have dated back to Roman times?

We are all aware that there is enough homophobic attitudes exist in today's current climate, and it only become legal for two consenting men to be together sexually in 1967 at first over the age of 21, hence the debate about gay rights moved too quickly for some, for some not quick enough for others. It still took decades to go from acceptance that homosexuality existed as part of the natural continuum to the position where gay marriage was legalised. Some have believed that during the first WW1 women become lesbians because there was a shortage of young men. But any gender specific people you talk to have already identified for a long time usually since early childhood that they have felt different about their own sexuality. Many can usually identify it at a young age, which leads us to believe that a person's sexuality is usually genetic and inherent from birth.

Intersex is a natural phenomenon known to the medical profession for centuries whereby a small percentage of humans are born with ambiguous reproductive organs. Persistent Mullerian Duct Syndrome, is the term for people born with male genitalia but also have female reproductive organs such as fallopian tubes or a uterus. In the USA it has been estimated that 1;2000 children are born with sexual organs that are indeterminate. It is therefore easy to consider and recognise that there are some people maybe born as one sex who sincerely feel and believe that they should be in the body of another. What has yet to be proven is how to make the leap beyond biology into personal testimony and the trans world may in the years to come be proven psychologically or biologically, this is appearing to be a scientific and social issue yet to be supported academically .

We believe that society might sanction individuals to act and behave in a certain way which may lead individuals to delay recognition of their own sexuality, due to cultural influences or family pressure that could stigmatise certain individuals. Some people believe the trans issue is delusional, but society should be encouraging individual agency as one effect of uncertainty in the UK has seen a 700% rise in child referrals to gender clinics in just 5 years. Could it be because if the child has strong gender related Autism in puberty, especially where we as a society now are hitting puberty younger and younger where the average age for a girl in puberty now is 10 years of age, her/his hormones are kicking in earlier and earlier and this can cause confusion especially when the individual does not have the mental capacity to understand what's happening to their bodies. Could this difference also be because we are more aware of gender differences, is it an online culture who push the issue? Some transbloggers who transition in real time and post their experiences have millions of followers and have become celebrities in their own right.

But where does sexuality and gender fit into the Autism Spectrum. Could it be that there is a lack of interconnectednesss usually associated with Autism?

In April 2015 the former Olympic Athlete and reality star to the Kardashian Family Bruce Jenner came out as a trans and revealed his new identity as Caitlyn Jenner and within weeks she was on the cover of Vanity Fair. But what happens if you know what gender you actually are and there is no lack of interconnectedness, that's fine too. That just means that your brain is wired slightly differently so that you prefer the companion of your choice regardless of sexuality, and many Autistics can look past a person's gender to see the character traits of that person that they are attracted to rather than the sex of the person.

Your endocrine system works with your nervous system to control important bodily functions. The endocrine systems responsibilities include regulating growth, sexual development and function, metabolism and mood. The endocrine system also helps give your body the energy it needs to function properly. Endocrine glands secrete hormones into the bloodstream. Hormones are considered chemical messengers, coordinating your body by transferring information from one set of cells to another. Your endocrine system health can be affected by hormone imbalances resulting from impaired glands. A hormone imbalance can cause problems with bodily growth, sexual development, metabolism and other bodily functions. Endocrine system diseases or conditions include diabetes, growth disorders and osteoporosis.

Although estrogens are thought of as female sex hormones and androgens are considered male hormones, both men and women make hormones in both groups, with different ratios depending on gender. For example, women make less than 10 percent of the amount of testosterone that men make. Testosterone is important in women for muscle and bone strength, and also for maintaining a healthy sex drive. Estrogen may play an important role in preventing heart disease in men. Younger men generally have higher levels of testosterone and lower levels of estrogen. With aging, estrogen levels often increase and testosterone levels decrease. This can lead to an increased risk of heart attacks, strokes, prostate enlargement, and prostate cancer in older men.

As society seems to dictate that there are more gender variations than ever before Heavy Metals can increase problems with hormones, especially mercury. Pesticides on crops we eat can influence our body's metabolism over generations and so can vaccinations. So over long periods of time our bodies metabolism has changed compared to our caveman days due to the changes in our diet of processed foods. Back in the 1990's Andrew Wakefield was very publicly defamed for stating that vaccinations were a cause for Autism. His career was ruined and he fled to America, which is where he still lives today his career was in tatters ruined by the British Government because it questioned validity of immunisations and the combination and number of vaccinations used on a child from birth. This speculation led to scores and scores of children not to be vaccinated by the triple vaccination Measles Mumps and Rubella. Subsequently news was made every time a child died of one of these child hood illness. The triple vaccination at that time contained an aluminium which helped stabilise and preserve the vaccine known as thiromersal and the levels of content in the vaccinations had a compound effect on Autism as it increased the metal content in a babies body. When thiromersal was discovered to be in the triple vaccinations it was promptly removed and other forms of preservative were to be used without the mental content. If you look at the fact that baby had close on to 15 injections in its first year. A babies body would be in overload. However it wasn't in the government's best interest to slow down the production of vaccinations especially when Jeremy Hunt the then current health minister sat on the board of directors for the joint vaccination committee, who also had a vested interest in the pharmaceutical industry along with many other politicians today who believe in vaccinations for immunity.

Over generations since, mercury and other metals sit in the reproductive organs of both men and women and this is what affects their hormone levels and subsequently affects their level of sexuality. It also contributes to the Autistic brain. As various brain scans show that an Autistic brain is far heavier metal content wise. Bearing this in mind, if we are all on the spectrum in varying degrees then by brain scan you could be able to tell by the level of metals in your brain. But technically science hasn't advanced that far yet. Andrew Wakefield did hit on a theory that more children were being diagnosed with Autism but it is both generational, genetic and down to the babies level of sensitivities when the vaccinations were given, it just happened to coincide all at the wrong time for Andrew and the speculation was covered up beyond any proportions imaginable.

As more and more genders and dysphoria is coming out into the open, some gender experiences can also be considered dissociative, where in an Autistic mind it forms part of a compartmentalisation. For this to make sense I will explain it further, when a child is sexually abused or raped the body can form a coping mechanism by disassociating from the traumatic experience kind of like looking down on itself from above, a form of detachment. This can also be similar to splitting as mentioned in the previous chapter on personality disorders. It's the bodies way of coping with a traumatic event. A separate dissociative identity forms as a coping mechanism and is usually known as a split personality and the individual can switch from one dissociative state to another without either personality being aware of the other, this can develop in extremely stressful times. There is a youtube video back from the 1950's who was filmed with three dissociative states Ms Black, Ms White and Ms Grey. Ms Grey was aware of both Ms Black and Ms White but Ms White and Ms Black did not know of each other. Ms Black was rather a loose morale woman back in the 1950's and Ms White was as her name suggests whiter than white. If you look at this example in its simplest form, some form of trauma caused her to develop a split personality. But not all trauma related incidents can cause a personality to split, or compartmentalise other factors as yet to be discovered by science can lead individuals to have multiple personalities as seen in the list of genders. Some dissociative identities can be vast, we have counselled one lady who had as many as 13 at one time. The Autistic brain has a way of splitting and compartmentalising, both in complex personality disorders, killers who adopt different personas who are not aware of the behaviour they have done, through lack of theory of mind and lack of self awareness and all these functions of the Autistic brain have similar characteristics in the way that the brain is wired. Disassociation by sleep walking is yet another example, where the person is not aware of the behaviour they are doing whilst asleep.

Lastly we would like to talk about Paedophilia as a sexual orientation. This might come as a shock to people reading this book, but sexual abuse and rape, and lets start with rape is a form of sexualised predatory behaviour, where the rapist does not take into account the feelings of the person. Like many of the personality disorders discussed in the previous chapter the rapist sole concern is with his one sided feelings of empowerment. The same can be said for Paedophilia, but paedophilia is a life style choice and form of sexuality, as paedophiles engage in sexual conduct with underage children and babies. Paedophilia or paedophilia is a psychiatric disorder in which an adult or older adolescent experiences a primary or exclusive sexual attraction to prepubescent children. The main cause is not known but linked to Abnormality in brain structure and function, Presence of certain neurological characteristics at birth, reduced levels of white matter, abuse in childhood by adults, comorbid psychiatric illnesses.

Studies of paedophilia in child sex offenders often report that it co-occurs with other psychopathologies, such as low self-esteem, depression, anxiety, and personality problems. This increases the likelihood that they will show psychological problems. Similarly, paedophiles convicted of a crime, making it more likely that they will show anti-social characteristics. Impaired self-concept and interpersonal functioning were reported in a sample of child sex offenders who met the diagnostic criteria for paedophilia where the most marked differences between paedophiles and controls were on the introversion scale, with paedophiles showing elevated shyness, sensitivity and depression. A review of qualitative research studies concluded that child sexual abusers use cognitive distortions to meet personal needs, justifying abuse by making excuses, redefining their actions as love and mutuality, and exploiting the power imbalance inherent in all adult–child relationships. Other cognitive distortions include the idea of "children as sexual beings", uncontrollability of sexual behaviour, and "sexual entitlement-bias". Consumption of child pornography is a more reliable indicator of paedophilia than molesting a child, although some non-paedophiles also view child pornography. Child pornography may be used for a variety of purposes, ranging from private sexual gratification or trading with other collectors, to preparing children for sexual abuse as part of the child grooming process.

You can argue that paedophilia is a genetic imbalance of the brain, genetic, a learned behaviour in families, generational or a mirrored behaviour, ie: I had it done to me as a child therefore I would go onto do it to children when I grow up. (I would like to add further that this rather naive ignorant and damaging viewpoint is still thought today that if you were sexually abused as a child you would go onto abuse others yourself including your own children). This cognitive impairment that causes paedophilia is not yet known, studies suggest that there are one or more neurological characteristics present at birth that cause or increase the likelihood of being paedophilic plus numerous other factors. There is no evidence that paedophilia can be cured. Instead, most therapies focus on helping the paedophile refrain from acting on their desires. Similarly many therapies have tried to cure men from being gay. The prevalence of paedophilia in the general population is not known, Less is known about the prevalence of paedophilia in women, but there are case reports of women with strong sexual fantasies and urges towards children. Most sexual offenders against children are male. Females may account for 0.4% to 4% of convicted sexual offenders, and one study estimates a 10 to 1 ratio of male-to-female child molesters.

Tony Attwood leading author on autism believes most controversially, society needs to tackle the taboo subject of ASD and paedophilia. Speaking ahead of World Autism Awareness Day today, he suggested that many inmates in sex offender units, including those convicted of child pornography offences, show signs of Asperger's or ASD. Autism is characterised by delayed social maturity and social reasoning, difficulty in forming relationships, problems with the communication and control of emotions, and fascination with a topic that is unusual in its intensity and which can become an obsession. "One of the things we need to do is work with the prison service," said Attwood. "People with Asperger's are not very good at forming relationships, so they may seek a relationship commensurate with their mental maturity, but it's illegal. Then pornography becomes a special interest. They download illegal pornography to complete the collection, not necessarily because they are a paedophile. "When I talked to prison staff at the sex offender unit, the light bulbs went on in relation to about half the people there having signs of Asperger's syndrome. "In law, it is possession of child pornography, not necessarily being a paedophile (which constitutes the offence). So when I talk to people with Asperger's about having an intimate relationship with a child, they often find it absolutely abhorrent. But because they are interested in pornography, and pressed the button to download it, they are then arrested." "It is about encouraging people to be aware of aspects of sexuality," he said. "The person is having physiological responses according to their physiological age, but they are not getting the genuine romantic experiences. We want them to have those, not to seek fulfilment on the internet. "We have developed programmes called the Dating Game and Beyond Friendship so that they can learn to have typical relationships rather than escape into imagination. Pornography will fill the imagination with inappropriate images. We need to work not just on friendships but beyond friendship." Parents and teachers must be reassured that a child who has a diagnosis of ASD will not grow up to be an offender, said Attwood. His view is supported by Dr Richard Curen, a consultant forensic psychotherapist with the charity Respond, which works with children and adults with learning disabilities who have experienced abuse or trauma, as well as those who have abused others. However people with stronger Autistic Spectrum conditions are more likely to be bullied, victimised, and sexually abused across all capacities sectors and environments, it's our job to recognise when this may be happening and causing an issue to those concerned.

However one key Autistic characteristic may have been over looked Autistics have a strong characteristic to mirroring behaviours. Mirroring is the behaviour in which one person subconsciously imitates the gesture, speech pattern, or attitude of another. Mirroring often occurs in social situations, particularly in the company of close friends intimate or family relationships. The concept often affects other individuals' notions about the individual that is exhibiting mirroring behaviours, which can lead to the individual building rapport with others. The display of mirroring often begins as early as infancy, as babies begin to mimic individuals around them and establish connections with particular body movements. The ability to mimic another person's actions allows the infant to establish a sense of empathy and thus begin to understand another person's emotions. The infant continues to establish connections with other individual's emotions and subsequently mirror their movements. In its simplest form – yawning by example can lead to other members of the group yawing and can be infectious. Controversial yet again it is said the mirror imaging neurons in autism are damaged, We believe this to not be the case as many people on the spectrum possess a lot of mirroring behaviours as we will look at this in other chapters especially in domestic abuse.

Chapter 7

Why Isn't Addiction On The Spectrum?

Classic hallmarks of addiction include impaired control over substances or behaviour, preoccupation with substance or behaviour, and continued fixation or habit of an activity despite all consequences. I would call these forms of behaviour an obsessive desire of power and controlling behaviour, where the consequences of this type of activity supersedes the thought process of anybody or anything else, where there is a complete lack of awareness of what the addictive behaviour is doing to those around them. Habits and patterns associated with addiction are typically characterised by immediate gratification (short-term reward), coupled with delayed deleterious effects (long-term costs). Moreover I would suggest there is a complete blind spot or lack of context to the addicts thinking - again it's the same thing we've talked about earlier called lack of theory of mind and context blindness to the actions of the addict. I would also like to say at this point that not all addictive behaviour can be negative. For example I have an addictive behaviour towards collecting glass and antique pottery, this can be seen as a healthy addiction or obsession, it is only when it becomes a negative and can take over my life where I could spend all my money and time on it insensitive to the consequences of my family and children putting my needs first to the detriment of others.

Some examples of negative addictions drug and behavioural include alcoholism, amphetamine addiction, cocaine addiction, nicotine addiction, opioid addiction, food addiction and associated food related behaviours, sugar, caffine etc, gambling addiction, shopping addiction, tabaco, cannabis, prescription drugs (sleeping pills, sedatives, hypnotics etc) inhalants, and sexual pornography addiction. Other addictions include - Playing video games, using a computer, work, exercise, pain, cutting (self harm), hoarding and spiritual as opposed to religious devotion.

Some people use the word disease, to describe the behaviours. The only behavioural addiction recognized by the DSM-5 manual and the ICD-10 is Gambling addiction. The term addiction is misused frequently to refer to other compulsive behaviours or disorders, particularly dependence. The DSM-5 lists disorders where impulses cannot be resisted, which could be considered a type of addiction. The following is a list of the recognised impulse control disorders: Intermittent explosive disorder (compulsive aggressive and assaultive acts), Kleptomania (compulsive stealing), Pyromania (compulsive setting of fires).

We believe control plays an important part. An important distinction between drug addiction and dependence is that drug dependence is a disorder in which cessation of substance or type of behaviour use results in an unpleasant state of withdrawal, which can lead to further use of the type of behaviour. Addiction is the compulsive use of a substance or performance of a behaviour that is independent of withdrawal. Addiction can occur in the absence of dependence, and dependence can occur in the absence of addiction, although the two often occur together.

We would also like to explain the difference between a street drug and a prescription drug. A drug sold illegally and used for its mood-altering, stimulant, or sedative effects is a street drug, a substance taken for nonmedical purposes. Street drugs comprise various amphetamines, anesthetics, barbiturates, opiates, and psychoactive drugs, and many are derived from natural sources (for example, the plants Papaver Somniferum, Cannibis Sativa, Amanita Pantherina, Lophophora williamsii). Slang names include acid (lysergic acid diethylamide), angel dust (phencyclidine), coke (cocaine), downers (barbiturates), grass (marijuana), hash (concentrated tetrahydrocannibinol), magic mushrooms (psilocybin), and speed (amphetamines). During the 1980s, a new class of "designer drugs" arose, mostly analogues of psychoactive substances intended to escape regulation under the Controlled Substances Act. Additionally, crack cocaine, a potent, smokable form of cocaine, emerged as a major public health problem. In the U.S., illicit use of drugs (for example, cocaine, marijuana, and heroin) has historically recurred in cycles. Even though alcohol is not classed as illegal, Consumed in quantities it is damaging to the body and its mind altering.

Where by a prescription drug is prescribed with a recommended daily dose, the difference between street drugs and prescription drugs is the user will self medicate and abuse the daily allowance. Most prescribed drugs are cleaner and purer in substances but this may not always be the case now due to generic cheaper versions of the same drugs. Prescription drugs are often dispensed together with a monograph (in Europe, a Patient Information Leaflet or PIL) that gives detailed information about the drug and often regulated and controlled substances. Even though a pharmaceutical drug that legally requires a medical prescription to be dispensed. In contrast, over-the-counter drugs can be obtained without a prescription. The reason for this difference in substance control is the potential scope of misuse, from drug abuse to practicing medicine without a license and without sufficient education. Different jurisdictions have different definitions of what constitutes a prescription drug. All mind altering drugs whether street or prescription drugs can be abused. Some examples of opioids include painkillers, codeine, fentanyl, morphine, oxymorphine, hydrocodone. Misuse includes taking a medication in a way or dose other than prescribed, taking someone else's medication, or taking the medicine so that it gives you an effect of getting high.

When addiction occurs with the use of a drug, it is more often than not the users need to quell or quieten the anxiety in mind with the substance, usually there is an indication of an underlying personality disorder as discussed in previous chapters, but the addict will often than not be able to regulate the amount of street drug required which is why useage gaps occur in an addict on street medication, as opposed to a user on prescribed medication ie: a binge drinker might only go on a bender every now and then because the substance used stays topped up in their system because they will over use the quantity for example consume excessive amounts in a small time scale. The executive functioning side of the brain, executive functions (collectively referred to as executive function and cognitive control) are a set of cognitive processes that are necessary for the cognitive control of behaviour: selecting and successfully monitoring behaviours that facilitate the attainment of chosen goals. Executive functions include basic cognitive processes such as attentional control, cognitive inhibition, inhibitory control, working memory, and cognitive flexibility. Higher order executive functions require the simultaneous use of multiple basic executive functions and include planning and fluid intelligence (e.g., reasoning and problem solving), will become effected especially over long term addiction use because they are being tampered with every time an addict uses and does not self prescribe the correct dosages as social reasoning behaviour becomes severely impaired as over dose occurs and the body and mind are unable to handle the quantities. The non use of boundary setting becomes clear along with the behaviour because cognitive functioning skills are not working correctly which is why the addictive behaviour is very similar to other autistic spectrum conditions which is why it needs to have its place on the spectrum recognised in its entirety.

Blame and denial are present in some form in all addictions. The beginning of recovery starts with seeing that "I" can do something to start to change. This is called a moment of clarity and does not happen often.

There are a number of genetic and environmental risk factors for developing an addiction that vary across the population. Genetic and environmental risk factors each account for roughly half of an individual's risk for developing an addiction; the contribution from epigenetic (Epigenetic changes modify the activation of certain genes, but not the genetic code sequence of DNA) risk factors to the total risk is unknown. Even in individuals with a relatively low genetic risk, exposure to sufficiently high doses of an addictive substance or type of behaviour for a long period of time (e.g., weeks–months) can result in an addiction. Epigenetics can best be described in simplistic terms as if a grandparent had a fear of dogs - the fear of dogs can be embedded in the gene code system and can be handed down through the gene link so the grandson can have a fear of dogs.

Compulsive shopping is characterised by excessive shopping that causes impairment in a person's life such as financial issues or not being able to commit to a family or other people as the compulsive shopping can take priority over everything else. The prevalence rate for this compulsive behaviour is 5.8% worldwide, and a majority of the people who suffer from this type of behaviour are women (approximately 80%). There is no proven treatment for this type of compulsive behaviour, although some forms of psycho therapy can reduce the desire and impulse.

Hoarding is characterised by excessive saving of possessions and having problems when throwing these belongings away. Major features of hoarding include not being able to use living quarters in the capacity of which it is meant, having difficulty moving throughout the home due to the massive amount of possessions, as well as having blocked exits that can pose a danger to the hoarder and their family and guests. Items that are typically saved by hoarders include clothes, newspapers, containers, junk mail, books, plastic bags, food and craft items. Hoarders believe these items will be useful in the future or they are too sentimental to throw away. Other reasons include fear of losing important documents, information and object characteristics.

Compulsive overeating is the inability to control the amount of nutritional intake, resulting in excessive weight gain. This overeating is usually a coping mechanism to deal with issues in the individual's life such as stress. Most compulsive over-eaters know that what they are doing is not good for them. The compulsive behaviour usually develops in early childhood. People who struggle with compulsive eating usually do not have proper coping skills to deal with the emotional issues that cause their overindulgence in food. They indulge in binges, periods of varying duration in which they eat and/or drink without pause until the compulsion passes or they are unable to consume any more. These binges are usually accompanied by feelings of guilt and shame about using food to avoid emotional stress. This compulsive behaviour can have deadly side effects including, but not limited to, binge eating; depression; withdrawal from activities due to weight; and spontaneous dieting. Though this is a very serious compulsive behaviour, getting treatment and a proper diet plan can help individuals overcome these behaviours.

We believe controlling behaviours are used as a coping mechanism so that the individual doing the controlling behaviour can feel safe, sometimes the behaviours start as a recreational activity and can then become an obsessive behaviour. A lot of addictive behaviour can also be routed in fantasy escapism and day dreaming about the obsessive behaviour is all part of it. Controlling behaviours for example coupled with food related issues gives the individual an obsessive control over their environment especially if everything else in their life is out of control, so to control what they eat or don't eat or purge for example gives them a sense of authority, and mastering of their environment because they feel powerless or worthless without it.

Compulsive gambling is characterised by having the desire to gamble and not being able to resist said desires. The gambling leads to serious personal and social issues in the individual's life. This compulsive behaviour usually begins in early adolescence for men and between the ages of 20-40 for women. People who have issues controlling compulsions to gamble usually have an even harder time resisting when they are having a stressful time in life. People who gamble compulsively tend to run into issues with family members, the law, and the places and people they gamble with. The majority of the issues with this compulsive behaviour are due to lack of money to continue gambling or pay off debt from previous gambling.

Professional gamblers poker players or blackjack for example have an excellent skill at reading people, whether this could be classed as an autistic trait very little publicised cases exist apart from the film Rain Man with Dustin Hoffman. Part of the Spectrum involves identifying patterns, numbers, colour sequences etc. If the player is adept at it they could develop a strategy that could be hard to beat. However the difference is between compulsive behaviour and playing for sport without the risk is that impulsive gambling can put the player at financial risk and the losses that are associated with gambling causes severe problems loosing a home, becoming a financial risk due to poor credit rating and excessive debt. Compulsive gambling can be helped with various forms of treatment such as Cognitive Behavioural Therapy, Self-help or Twelve-step programs, and potentially medication.

Trichotillomania and skin picking, Trichotillomania is classified as compulsive picking of hair of the body. It can be from any place on the body that has hair. This picking results in bald spots. Most people who have mild Trichotillomania can overcome it via concentration and more self-awareness. Those that suffer from compulsive skin picking have issues with picking, rubbing, digging, or scratching the skin. These activities are usually to get rid of unwanted blemishes or marks on the skin. These compulsions also tend to leave abrasions and irritation on the skin. This can lead to infection or other issues in healing. These acts tend to be prevalent in times of anxiety, boredom, or stress.

Checking, counting, washing, and repeating again is a form of addictive behaviour Compulsive checking can include compulsively checking items such as locks, switches, and appliances. This type of compulsion usually deals with checking whether harm to oneself or others is possible. Usually, most checking behaviours occur due to wanting to keep others and the individual safe. People that suffer from compulsive counting tend to have a specific number that is of importance in the situation they are in. When a number is considered significant, the individual has a desire to do the behaviour such as wiping ones face off the number of times that is significant. Compulsive counting can include instances of counting things such as steps, items, behaviours, and mental counting. It can also be applied to religions and used in forms of repetitive prayer or praying rituals. Compulsive repeating is characterised by doing the same activity multiple times over. These activities can include re-reading a part of a book multiple times, re-writing something multiple times, repeating routine activities, or saying the same phrase over and over. Compulsive washing is usually found in individuals that have a fear of contamination. People that have compulsive hand washing behaviours wash their hands repeatedly throughout the day. These hand washings can be ritualised and follow a pattern. People that have problems with compulsive hand washing tend to have problems with chapped or red hands due to the excessive amount of washing done each day.

Sexual and pornographic this type of compulsive behaviour is characterised by feelings, thoughts, and behaviours about anything related to sex. These thoughts have to be pervasive and cause problems in health, occupation, socialisation, or other parts of life. These feelings, thoughts, and behaviours can include normal sexual behaviours or behaviours that are considered illegal and/or morally and culturally unacceptable. This disorder is also known as hyper sexuality, hyper sexual disorder, nymphomania, voyeurism, or sexual addiction. Controversially, some scientists have characterised compulsive sexual behaviour as sexual addiction, although no such condition is recognised by mainstream medical diagnostic manuals.

Talking compulsive talk goes beyond the bounds of what is considered to be a socially acceptable amount of talking. The two main factors in determining if someone is a compulsive talker are talking in a continuous manner, only stopping when the other person starts talking, and others perceiving their talking as a problem. Personality traits that have been positively linked to this compulsion include assertiveness, willingness to communicate, self-perceived communication competence, and neuroticism. Studies have shown that most people who are talkaholics are aware of the amount of talking they do, are unable to stop, and do not see it as a problem

So how does an addictive behaviour relate to autism? Autism and Alcoholism are now genetically linked for the first time, a gene that carries an increased risk of Autism has also been associated with Alcoholism by scientists. Alcoholism can be linked to a gene that also causes Autism, found a recent study conducted in London. "A gene called Autism Susceptibility Candidate 2 (AUTS2) was associated with alcoholism," reported FYI Living. The study which gathered data from 26,316 participants from 12 European populations tracked how much alcohol each person consumed daily. The subjects' DNA was then examined for the AUTS2 gene. The researchers also used boozing mice to find out whether rodents with the AUTS2 gene hit the bottle harder: "A statistically significant association between amounts of alcohol consumed and AUTS2 gene expression was noted." So yes the gene was found to be present in a higher-than-average number of alcoholic mice, as well as people. Scientists estimate that around 40% of alcoholics carry a genetic predisposition to their addiction. The study isn't the first to note a high incidence of alcoholism in families with Autism, but the genetic evidence it uncovered is new. It's hoped that the latest discoveries will aid understanding of the hereditary mechanisms that influence both alcoholism and Autism.

A twin studies highlight the significant role genetics play in addiction. Twins have similar and sometimes identical genetics. Analysing these genes in relation to genetics has helped geneticists understand how much of a role genes play in addiction. Studies performed on twins found that rarely did only one twin have an addiction. In most cases where at least one twin suffered from an addiction, both did, and often to the same substance. Cross addiction is when already has a predisposed addiction and then starts to become addicted to something different. If one family member has a history of addiction, the chances of a relative or close family developing those same habits are much higher than one who has not been introduced to addiction at a young age.

In a separate recent study done by the National Institute on Drug Abuse, from 2002 to 2017, overdose deaths have almost tripled amongst male and females. In 2017, 72,306 overdose deaths happened in the U.S. that were reported.

Other family links to Autism and its traits is likely that if one family member is an addict other siblings, first cousins, aunts and uncles are likely to exhibit the same or similar tendencies. At present research is very limited however scientists believe that gene changes are a likely cause to autism that runs in families, 'risk' genes tend to look very different in families where family members may have different problems and challenges so the spectrum traits may look differently but lots of questions still remain (Goodman 2015). Like wise if one family member has a diagnosis on the Spectrum it is with doubt other family members could carry some of the autistic traits they just have not be classified in the medical manuals yet to have them all linked. We would say that you would be extremely naive if you did not have family who had traits of the Autism Spectrum unless you were an only adopted child.

Drawing from our own research on addiction in neuroscience, psychology, and clinical practice, the following list identifies several key behavioural patterns associated with addiction:

There are many unsuccessful attempts to quit. Addicts often express a desire to quit completely, but are unable to follow through. Short-term abstention is common, but long-term relapse rates are high. As Mark Twain said about the pains of quitting smoking: "It's easy. Done it a thousand times."

There are cue-triggered relapses, experience with an addictive substance sensitises the user to environmental cues that subsequently trigger cravings. These cues (e.g., clinking ice cubes) signal opportunities for consumption. For example, upon exiting rehab, addicts who return to their old environment are more likely to experience cravings and resume use. A recovering addict is also significantly more likely to "fall off the wagon" if he receives a small taste of his drug of choice or experiences stress. This is the very phenomenon that AA warns of, that abstinent alcoholics can't resume occasional drinking without losing control this is a very real risk.

Experience of a loss of control - Loss of control means that one is knowingly acting against their prior determination to abstain for example, consuming a larger portion of dessert after deciding to go on a diet. The typical reaction to this failure involves strong negative emotions (e.g., depression and self-loathing). It is instructive that the twelve-step program of Alcoholic Anonymous begins, "We admit we are powerless over alcohol - that our lives have become unmanageable." We hope that AA approach applies to more than just some.

There is often desire without pleasure where addicts commonly continue their behaviour even while reporting that the substance (e.g.,cigarette or drink) is no longer a pleasurable experience. Addicts often express that they continue to use drugs even when they no longer derive any pleasure. For example, some cigarette smokers express a deep hatred of smoking, but they continue to smoke regularly.

Staying vigilant despite the development of some effective treatments, at present there is no full proof cure for addiction. Recovering addicts often manage their tendency to make mistakes by exercising cognitive control, such as voluntarily reducing or eliminating future options. The main purpose is to reduce the probability of encountering cues that will trigger relapse. For example, even addicts who have stayed clean for years attend meetings of support groups / settings in which no individual therapies or drugs are provided some are based on 12 step spiritual programmes. AA one of the leading pioneers in the support group field helps decrease the likelihood of long term progressive drinking. We believe that all addicts need some form of support, even if they manage successfully to kick the addictive behaviour. Without dealing with the underlying issue in the first place whether it be anxiety, depression, a life event, or an underlying personality issue or sometimes no explanation at all, continued support will always be needed not to reoccur again.

Cross-addiction can occur where many addicts often substitute one compulsive problem for another. They become compulsive workers or gamblers, or use sex as they once used chemicals to combat the emptiness, boredom, anxiety, and depression that constantly threaten to overwhelm them. The self-medication theory of addiction suggests that individuals with deficits in emotion-regulation skills - the skills relevant for modifying emotional reactions and tolerating negative emotions - may use addictive behaviours in an attempt to manage negative or distressing affective states. For instance, individuals with histories of exposure to adverse childhood environments (e.g., physical and sexual abuse) tend to have a diminished capacity to regulate negative emotions and cope effectively with stress.

Genetic vulnerability where most individuals who try drugs use them only a few times, some will never advance beyond experimentation. Others will quickly become deeply involved and stay that way for a long time. There is substantial evidence of a genetic predisposition to develop an addiction. For example, due to genetic vulnerability, children of alcoholics are at higher risk for future alcohol problems, and many show high levels of impulsivity. Thus, you may have two glasses of wine and desire no more, and yet a genetically vulnerable person struggles to stop with six. It's about having an awareness that both a learned or environmental behaviour plus having a pre disposition to the effects of possibly becoming addict all play their part in its progression.

Is there a difference between a substance abuser and an addict? At some undefined point, substance abusers are no longer in control of their substance use. Just as a pickle can never become a cucumber again, once a person crosses over this undefined line, there is an alteration in brain circuitry that cannot be reversed. Every drug addict starts out as an occasional user and then shifts to a compulsive user. Depending on the substance used and or what it is used with.

Addiction is not limited to substance abuse, the psychological concept of operant conditioning suggests that if a behaviour is followed by a rewarding experience, an animal (or individual) becomes more likely to repeat the rewarding behaviour at a later time. For example, a dog performs a trick to get a dog treat. In human beings, operant conditioning allows them to learn behaviour leading to certain rewards (or consequences). For example, learning that playing video games (or web-surfing, shopping, or work) is followed by a reduction in distress, an individual will be more likely to engage in the act in the future.

The reaction gives a reward in some way e.g. a child that wants its mother's attention can do so by yelling at her. The mother then wants the kid to stop yelling and gives the child attention. Doing so teaches the child that as a reward to yelling it gets mum's attention but as we know yelling however is not a social accepted means of communication. So reverse conditioning this behaviour could be that the mother spanks the child when it starts yelling. Since the child then still gets attention it will most likely continue to yell, even though the "reward" is a negative one, it can still be interpreted as "getting attention". So this way most likely will not work. Another way of "unlearning" this behaviour is completely ignoring the child when it starts yelling. This requires some control over your own behaviour. Especially when a kid yells at mum in a supermarket, throws itself to the floor and cries like the end of the world is near, you need to stay firm. When the child then becomes aware that no matter how hard it yells and cries it will not get the attention from the mother it will maybe sob for a while but it will eventually come to mum and ask in a different, more acceptable, way for attention, e.g. simply asking. The mother then can answer the question/request of the child. If mother keeps that attitude of ignoring the yelling and replying to the normal question the child will then learn that yelling doesn't give the wanted reaction (it is ignored) and that asking a normal question WILL give a reward (a positive one) and thus it will use that strategy in the future.

This is not much different from animals. In dog training several years ago it was a normal way to "punish" the dog for misbehaviour. However, this punishment was a "reward" as well. The dog did get attention from its owner. In today's training methods the positive approach is more effective. When a dog does something it is not allowed to do it is ignored. As soon as it behaves the way we expect it to do we reward it. We can give the dog a small snack, or stroke it or show our enthusiasm.

You have to repeat this several times and even hundreds of times before addicts get the hang of it if at all. Typical human behaviour, if something doesn't work try it again, but harder this time, ignoring the fact that the first time the behaviour did not bring the desired result... In extreme cases behaviour never changes and autistics may never learn via reverse conditioning and consequences of their behaviour because their neural pathways and cognitions do not accept or are not equipped to re route the new information, and that is something we have to learn to accept. Once we learn to accept then this can bring a whole set of relief that we can't change another person's behaviour, the only behaviour we can change is our own.

But are Asperger's, Autism and Addiction actually related? With these symptoms in mind; Autism and addictive behaviour is not commonly reported or scientifically proven as yet. However, those with high functioning Asperger's or Autism may find self medicating with addictive behaviour alleviates their anxiety. Social situations are often extremely stressful for those that fall in this spectrum. One form of 'dual diagnosis' is often used to treat those with an addiction, it's also useful to find other mental health conditions, the comorbidity of addictive behaviour disorders and mental health conditions is pretty high. Addictive behaviours are very common in those with Asperger's and Autism Spectrum Disorder. Children and adults with ADHD also fall into addictive patterns. The real problem here is self medication, while the relationship between Asperger's autism and addiction is less likely; the common practice of self medicating does extend into those with the diagnosis of Autism Spectrum Disorder and Asperger's. Even those with ADHD fall into self medicating cycles when they find it alleviates the anxiety and stress associated with their mental health. Self medicating can be a practice of self harm when not done with the guidance of medical professionals. Schizophrenia and drug abuse are very common. Many people with Schizophrenia look to substances to self medicate and ease their symptoms. There are legitimate chemical imbalances found in those with depression, anxiety, ADHD and Autism Spectrum Disorder and a great deal of research has been conducted to understand the full extent of mental health conditions and the impact on the brain.

One thing that is certain is that the chemicals inside of the brain are not being released or functioning as they would in those without symptoms indicating a mental health condition. What this means is that other substances can help replicate normal function to aid in helping those with mental health conditions maintain normal function. Just like other health conditions inhibit normal functions; medication is used to help those that need it to carry out a more comfortable life. Self medicating may seem like a cost effective route to feeling better, but it may cause more harm than good. Replacing one bad thing with another doesn't get you ahead, it just puts another barrier in the way to recover.

Once a formal diagnosis is given and proper treatment is received, it is easier to understand your own bodies unique function. While a diagnosis may tell us something about you, the experiences that you have, the genetics you possess and your own unique personality are things that no text book can teach a doctor. But with the correct training and proper understanding, these professionals can learn to understand your own unique needs and find ways to help you heal and recovery.

The practice and success of dual diagnosis is very integrated into personalised treatment. While most can find similarities between one person and another, each individual is unique. We all have experiences and other factors that make us different. Between medical interventions and therapy the process of recovery is really aided by focusing on each person with all of the symptoms associated, there are definitely instances where the two go together. Finding help for symptoms that involve depression, anxiety and stress can aid in recovery from addictive behaviour or prevent the use of substances and unhealthy coping strategies to self medicate.

Let's hope in the near future Scientists are able to link all other forms of addiction obsessive behaviour and hopefully things might change in the way that we view addictive behaviour.

Chapter 8

Domestic Abuse, Why Isn't It On The Spectrum?

Domestic Abuse has previously been explored but not in connection with people on the autistic spectrum in any depth and there is a lot to learn from people with autism. Currently there is a gap in our knowledge base and at the moment it is a tentative connection and could be extremely productive if researched, at present recent figures from Women's Aid UK state 1-3 women experience domestic abuse in their lifetime as do 1-5 men.

As discussed in the previous chapter about executive functioning impairments executive brain functions (collectively referred to as executive function and cognitive control) are a set of brain processes that are necessary for the cognitive control of behaviour: especially in autism when selecting and successfully monitoring behaviours that facilitate the attainment of chosen goals.

Executive brain functions include basic brain cognitive processes such as attentional control, cognitive inhibition, inhibitory control, working memory, and cognitive flexibility. Higher order executive brain functions require the simultaneous use of multiple basic executive functions and include planning and fluid intelligence (e.g., reasoning and problem solving). Cognitive control and stimulus control, which is associated with operant and classical conditioning.

(Classical conditioning involves making an association between an involuntary response and a stimulus, while operant conditioning is about making an association between a voluntary behaviour and a consequence. In operant conditioning, the learner is also rewarded with incentives, while classical conditioning involves no such enticements). Compete the overall control of an individual's elicited behaviours.

What we do already know from science is that cognitive brain control is impaired in addiction, attention deficit hyperactivity disorder, autism, and associated conditions and a number of other central nervous system disorders. Impaired means reduced, lessened, compromised, or damaged. But how can an impaired brain cognitive function be damaged when individuals who displays these character traits seem to function highly intelligently? Well, as I suggested earlier, it means that they can function highly in one area, but lack insight in another area often to their detriment or the detriment of others.

For example stimulus-driven behavioural responses that are associated with a particular rewarding stimulus tend to dominate one's behaviour; for example, in addiction – ie: a person craves a substance and will do everything he can to get hold of it even when money runs out even if that includes robbery, all rational thought of the damage he is doing to others goes out of the window for his stimulus driven behaviour. A person who does not think in this way will see it as crazy, irrational behaviour, but to the person with a cognitive brain impairment he sees it only through his lens. Could the same be applied to the way one behaves about domestic abusive behaviour, do they see it as rewarding?

Domestic abusive behaviour in men and women is now more than ever in the spot light due to more high profile cases in the media and as we develop more understanding of its complex nature and, in a kind of inverted gas lighting, (gaslighting definition is the action of tricking or controlling someone by making them believe things that are not true, especially by suggesting that they may be mentally ill). Perpetrators began to describe victims as having Autism as a way of controlling their spouses and the Autistic thinking and behaviour patterns are very much found when working in domestic violence settings within agencies working with clients, perpetrators and victims. So should Domestic abuse be considered an impaired memory function, a fault with the executive function of the brain and cognitive memory.

Coercive Control is a sustained pattern of domestic abusive behaviour, or an emotional abusive situation where the abuser can be explained as having an Autistic brain to not to be able to see the other person's perspective or insight into one's own controlling behaviour that they impose on another individual.

The UK government's new coercive or controlling behaviour offence in Dec 2015 means victims who experience the type of behaviour that stops short and can include serious physical violence, but amounts to extreme psychological and emotional abuse, can now since 2015 bring their perpetrators to justice. The offence carries a maximum of 5 years' imprisonment, a fine or both. The coercive or controlling behaviour offence will protect victims who would otherwise be subjected to sustained patterns of abuse that can lead to total control of their lives by the perpetrator. Clare's Law memorialised Clare Wood who was killed in 2009 by an ex-partner who, unknown to her, had been violent to previous partners, The Domestic Violence Disclosure scheme was created in 2014, and gives an individual the right to ask the police to check if a partner has a history of abuse.

Coercive or controlling behaviour does not relate to a single incident, it is a purposeful pattern of incidents that occur over time in order for one individual to exert power, control or coercion over another during a relationship between intimate partners, former partners who still live together, or family members. Controlling behaviour is a range of acts designed to make a person subordinate and/or dependent by isolating them from sources of support, exploiting their resources and capacities for personal gain, depriving them of the means needed for independence, resistance and escape and regulating their everyday behaviour.

Some more specific examples include: Isolating a person from their friends and family, depriving them of their basic needs, monitoring their time, monitoring a person via online communication tools or using spyware, taking control over aspects of their everyday life, such as where they can go, who they can see, what to wear and when they can sleep, depriving them access to support services, such as specialist support or medical services, repeatedly putting them down such as telling them they are worthless, enforcing rules and activity which humiliate, degrade or dehumanise the victim, forcing the victim to take part in criminal activity such as shoplifting, neglect or abuse of children to encourage self-blame and prevent disclosure to authorities, financial abuse including control of finances, such as only allowing a person a punitive allowance, controlling the ability to go to school or place of study, taking wages, benefits or allowances, threats to hurt or kill, threats to harm a child, threats to reveal or publish private information (e.g. threatening to 'out' someone), threats to hurt or physically harming a family pet assault, criminal damage (such as destruction of household goods) preventing a person from having access to transport or from working, preventing a person from being able to attend school, college or University, family 'dishonour', reputational damage, disclosure of sexual orientation, disclosure of HIV status or other medical condition without consent, limiting access to family, friends and finances.

This is not an exhaustive list and you should be aware that a perpetrator will often tailor the conduct to the victim, and that this conduct can vary to a high degree from one person to the next. In many relationships, there are occasions when one person makes a decision on behalf of another, or when one partner takes control of a situation and the other has to compromise. The difference in an abusive relationship is that decisions by a dominant partner can become rules that, when broken, lead to consequences for the victim, such as enforced sexual activity including rape.

Domestic Abusive behaviour has yet to be formally linked in the DSM V manual of diagnostic criteria for Autism even though all the acts of behaviour can be linked to a 'Lack of Theory of Mind'. Theory of Mind is the ability to attribute mental states - beliefs, intents, desires, emotions, knowledge, etc, to oneself, and to others, and to understand that others have beliefs, desires, intentions, and perspectives that are different from one's own. Theory of mind is crucial for everyday human social interactions and is used when analysing, judging, and inferring others' behaviours. Deficits can occur in people with Autism Spectrum Disorders. Although not formally linked yet through science a clear recognition of the patterns is similar to a cognitive impairment of the executive functioning sides of the brain.

In 1985 Simon Baron-Cohen, Alan M. Leslie and Uta Frith suggested that children or adults with Autism do not employ theory of mind and suggested that autistic children and adults have particular difficulties with tasks requiring the child to understand another person's beliefs. In Domestic abuse the abuser finds it very difficult to see the victims perspective and in many incidences portrays themselves as the victim when challenged. They often will accuse the victim of what they are guilty of themselves in a clear sign of inverted thinking.

Like wise a victim of domestic abuse can both mirror the learnt behaviour from the perpetrator and can become an abuser themselves in relationships, not being able to see the bigger picture the controlling partner has imposed and they can be unable to think of a solution to get out of the abused environment because they have become conditioned, being acclimatised to his/her situation through lack of theory of mind or similarly a learnt behaviour, which suggests that with an Autistic person, deficits in theory of mind result from a distortion in understanding and responding to emotions.

Many victims of Domestic Abuse can and do identify with Stockholm Syndrome - Victims of the formal definition of Stockholm Syndrome develop "positive feelings toward their captors and sympathy for their causes and goals, and negative feelings toward the police or authorities". These symptoms often follow escaped victims back into their previously ordinary lives. The physical and psychological effects include Cognitive: confusion, blurred memory, refusal to accept the reality of events and recurring flashbacks. Emotional effects include lack of feeling, fear, helplessness, hopelessness, aggression, depression, guilt, dependence on captor and development of post-traumatic stress disorder (PTSD). Social: anxiety, irritability, cautiousness and estrangement. Physical effects include increase in effects of pre-existing conditions; development of health conditions due to possible restriction from food, sleep, and exposure to the outdoors.

Domestic abuse can often be a learnt behaviour, learnt behaviour is reproducing a behaviour a person has grown up in, and is more likely to be reproduced in adult hood. If a person has grown up in domestic abuse they can become a victim or perpetrator in adult life - for example if a person always has a roast dinner on a Sunday and Sundays were special family days, as the person grows up Sundays will always be special days in their family life now probably reproducing the Sunday Roast on a Sunday. Now using that example look at the previous examples of behaviour that could become a learnt behaviour such as watching your parents or grandparents addictive compulsive behaviour. It may also become your learnt behaviour as well where your autistic thinking brain kicks in because it is repetitive, comfortable and familiar behaviour.

If a person has grown up in an abusive home where one or more parent was abusive this will have an impact on that person as they grow up and they may well go on to copy that behaviour in their own relationship as an adult sometimes being aware of it, sometimes not being aware of it but being familiar with the behaviours makes it normal, comfortable and familiar. Having a conscious memory and often being powerless to change the dynamics of it happening is a learnt behaviour pattern from childhood.

Sometimes abusers go onto have multiple relationships where they are in power and control of a submissive partner and many victims may go on to have many abusive partners. This is known as a cyclical behaviour pattern where the cognitive functions of the brain have been rewired since childhood to accept this type of behaviour (learnt) or to carry this type of behaviour out as normal or normalised.

Having this cognitive disability of poor or faulty brain re wiring in the executive functioning side of the brain, where you do not recognise these patterns of abusive/self abusive destructive behaviour - with a lack of ability to recognise the faulty thought processes is very similar to a lack of context or theory of mind as discussed earlier in this book.

It can also be the effects of the autistic brain and its development from birth, in a lack of theory of mind where a child is pre disposed to aggressive angry outbursts from childhood progressing into adult hood and not being recognised, dealt with effectively or managed appropriately via medication or disciplined boundaries where there is a complete lack of consequences managed for the behaviour. Children who are looked after by a non abusive parent who provides good parenting and offers reassurance love and firm boundaries in a non aggressive way, can reduce the likelihood of the past exposure continuing on in the domestic abuse cycle of violence.

Some children who have PDA (Patheological Demand Avoidance) do have aggressive tendencies and physical outbursts. Is this a build up of frustration because they are unable to recognise and deal with emotion appropriately or is this there way of handling life if they feel overwhelmed? Passive aggressive behaviour is not acceptable in any form. The key is first to identify it and then to learn what the anxiety triggers could actually be.

However David Schnarch, a Colorado-based couples therapist. Argues an opposing viewpoint "Having Asperger's like syndrome does not give you Asperger's," says "Having a big belly does not make you pregnant. I've not seen a single case of what I would consider to be diagnosable Asperger's. But I have seen any number of cases of wives accusing husbands of it, any number of cases of husbands claiming to have it." It's the new ADHD, he says. "The wife doesn't want to accept that the husband knows what he's doing when he's doing something she doesn't like." Schnarch recalls a man who phoned him the day before a scheduled initial couples session and announced that he'd just been diagnosed with Asperger's. "As soon as this happened," Schnarch says, "I knew I had difficulty." He contacted the referring therapist, who said he'd suspected the man had Asperger's because he said things to his girlfriend that were so cruel he couldn't possibly understand their impact. As far as Schnarch was concerned, it was an all too familiar instance of sadism masquerading as disability. As yet being a perpetrator and its link to Domestic Violence and Abusive behaviour have yet to find themselves a place on the Autistic Spectrum.

Some abusive behaviour may not be learnt behaviour but can stem from birth or genetics for example as mentioned before the Autistic Spectrum Condition Pathological Demand Avoidance does have aggressive tendencies in its individuals but not everyone with PDA has aggressive behaviour, however studies and research into the condition is still taking place as this is a relatively new association to the Spectrum. Children and adults in meltdown and crisis mode are more likely to hit out with aggressive behaviours which need to be delt with appropriately or more young children will grow up to become perpetrators. PDA also use a lot of manipulation and control tactics because the world is scary place for them because they are demand avoidant, oversensitive to the demands of everyday life they feel the need to take control to filter what demands they can and can't do. Later in adult life this can be seen as manipulative controlling behaviour as life is all on their terms regardless of what others needs may be.

As more immigrants come into the UK they bring with them an ideology or mind set which is appropriate to their home country and they are not familiar with UK laws regarding domestic abuse, honour based violence (HBV) or female genital mutilation (FGM). Many of the mind sets are fixed ingrained learnt behaviours customs or traditions from their cultural back grounds which are not applicable to continue on in that mindset here in the UK. Multi agency work supports (MARAC) high risk individuals and agency work for the victim and perpetrator is vital so that an understanding of change of behaviour patterns is key, but lack of government funding resources, shelters and refuges is limited and despite Theresa Mays 2016 well meant plans when she became Prime Minister, the actual number of homicides cases are increasing per month compared to the number of support services that are out there and the ability for people to adhere to the capacity for change is a continual up hill battle.

Ideology and Domestic Abuse where does that sit at present many people are still stigmatised and hold the viewpoint that it is still acceptable form of behaviour, largely due to lack of education, slowness of society to change its belief system, cultural influences and learnt systemic behaviour. Domestic Abuse can be seen as no more common in countries where cultural 'justification' it may violate the countries laws and its main religious traditions.

Initially it was thought men are the abusers and women were the victims, as more and more research is done we now know that men can be victims too to DV from female perpetrators. Unfortunately a gender neutral approach is key where social systems give power to men and see women as the underdog, until society changes its outlook we have a long way to go to change ideology.

Terrorism extremism is an action or threat designed to influence the government or intimidate the public. This is larger scale mass domestic abuse of power and control in extreme forms. Its purpose is to advance a political, religious or ideological cause. The current UK definition of terrorism is given in the Terrorism Act 2006. In the UK we define terrorism as a violent action that: Endangers a person's life, other than that of the person committing the action, Involves serious violence against a person, causes serious damage to property, creates a serious risk to the public's health and safety, and or interferes with or seriously disrupts an electronic system. But how does terrorism differ from extremism? The Counter Extremism Strategy 2015 says: "Extremism is the vocal or active opposition to our fundamental values, including democracy, the rule of law, individual liberty, and respect and tolerance for different faiths and beliefs. We also regard calls for the death of members of our armed forces as extremist." It's important to remember that not all extremist groups, whether Islamist, far-right or other, will commit terrorist or violent acts. However, some groups pose particular threats, both online and offline. Underpinning the radicalisation process is an extremist ideology that seems appealing and credible, often because it appears to make sense of the young person's feelings of grievance or injustice. Personal vulnerabilities or local factors can make a young person more susceptible to extremist messages. These may include; sense of not belonging, behavioural problems, issues at home, lack of self-esteem, criminal activity, being involved with gangs. Children don't need to meet people to fall for their extremist beliefs. The internet is increasingly being used by extremist groups to radicalise young people. These groups will often offer solutions to feelings of being misunderstood, not listened to, or being treated unfairly.

We feel that It is important to caution here that there is no substantial link between ASD and terrorism. However, there may be specific risk factors which could increase the risk of offending among people with ASD. Autistic special interests such as fantasy, obsessiveness (extreme compulsiveness), the need for routine/predictability and social/communication difficulties can all increase the vulnerability of an person with ASD to going down the pathway to terrorism. Searching for a "need to matter", belong or social connection and support for someone who is alienated or without friends may also present as risk factors. People with an ASD may be more vulnerable to being drawn into increasingly more involved commitment. They also have a tendency to hyper focus in on their fascinations and interests at the expense of other attachments and life interests.

These are potentially the conditions which extremists are increasingly exploiting in people they target for recruitment and training. There is a clear need for clinicians carrying out forensic evaluations of people who have engaged in terror related actions to investigate whether ASD may be related to their behaviour. Such evaluations are vital not just in delivering justice - but also to ensure rehabilitation and offender management are informed by an understanding of the ASD diagnosis in each case. Are these acts of violence just a very simple case of black and white (dichotomous) thinking that many Autistics possess, where brain damage lack of executive brain function enables them to actually not consider any shades of grey in there thought process such as a form of emotion to the suffering and extent of the damage their activities will incur. I believe that brainwashing, ignorance, vulnerability, idealism and lack of social structure regularity and routine that many autistics need in order to function plays a role in attracting people to this ideology and society should be putting greater importance in understanding how brain development or dysfunction works to the advancement or detriment of society.

Domestic Abuse can take different forms in the way of sexual abuse, Harvey Weinstein paid off sexual harassment accusers for decades, three decades ago, the Hollywood producer Harvey Weinstein invited Ashley Judd to the Peninsula Beverly Hills hotel for what the young actress expected to be a business breakfast meeting. Instead, he had her sent up to his room, where he appeared in a bathrobe and asked if he could give her a massage or she could watch him shower. An investigation by The New York Times found previously undisclosed allegations against Mr.Weinstein stretching over nearly three decades, documented through interviews with current and former employees and film industry workers, as well as legal records, emails and internal documents from the businesses he has run, Miramax and the Weinstein Company. During that time, after being confronted with allegations including sexual harassment and unwanted physical contact, Mr. Weinstein had reached at least eight settlements with women, according to two company officials speaking on the condition of anonymity. In a statement to The Times Mr. Weinstein said: "I appreciate the way I've behaved with colleagues in the past has caused a lot of pain, and I sincerely apologize for it. Though I'm trying to do better, I know I have a long way to go." He added that he was working with therapists and planning to take a leave of absence to "deal with this issue head on."

The Weinstein furore sparked international outrage as many more women came forward who Weinstein had sexually harassed abusing both his power and position and internationally it sparked the # Me too Campaign - never take no for an answer. Mr Weinsteins lawyers stated "he denied many of the accusations as patently false." In comments to The Times earlier this week, Mr. Weinstein said that many claims in Ms. O'Connor's memo were "off base" and that they had parted on good terms. This clearly shows huge denial on Mr Weinsteins part, large ego centric nature and narcissistic behaviour had failed to accept responsibility for the damage he had caused so many women, failure to understand how women saw his behaviour as a gross misconduct, breach of power trust and degrading. A number of forced rapes which to his belief were consensual sex, indicates his lack of emotional context and lack of theory of mind contextual to the situation. A prolific clever businessman building a business from scratch, but lacked the emotional processes needed to understanding unacceptable behaviour. Weinstein's behaviour was repetitive and in an undercover honey trap set up by the New York Times when asking the undercover journalist to remove her top he stated on tape "this is what Iam used too" which clearly indicates obsessive repetitive harassing behaviour. Mr. Weinstein was a volcanic personality, given to fits of rage and personal lashings of male and female employees alike.

Ms. Bloom, who has been advising Mr. Weinstein over the last year on gender and power dynamics, called him "an old dinosaur learning new ways." She said she had "explained to him that due to the power difference between a major studio head like him and most others in the industry, whatever his motives, some of his words and behaviours can be perceived as inappropriate, even intimidating." which clearly indicates that he had no emotional reasoning or understanding the consequences of his actions when he was coercively bargaining young actresses into compromising sexual situations in lieu of a script reading or acting part. which is a clear indicator of domestic abuse to women. The #Me Too Campaign - has brought worldwide recognition to sexual abusive power at work, sociopathic behaviour is wide spread amongst the population but only extreme high profile cases become recognised worldwide. Let's hope this brings changes to future generations.

People with Autism have been known to get involved in stalking and one of the reasons that persons with Autism Spectrum Disorders are predisposed to stalking according to Tom Berney a U.K. Psychiatrist is that they have impaired perception of social signals, misinterpretation of rules, misinterpretation of relationships, lack of awareness or concern for the outcome, and a focussed obsessive interest. While this occurs it is not common. Sexually motivated crimes are also unusual and when they occur may be a consequence of a lack of understanding on the part of the person with Autism or ASD. ASD people may be aggressive and commit offences against other people, but it is unclear how frequently and what proportion of people are at risk of doing so. Many people on the spectrum have a hypertrophied sense of right and wrong and are unusually conscientious and unwilling to break the law. They are more likely to be victims than perpetrators. Nevertheless even though it is uncommon persistent violence by a person with ASD is a particularly difficult problem. Violence by a person with ASD often has some special features. It may be triggered by idiosyncratic stimuli nourished by rumination over past slights; displaced from provoking the person onto a safer target at a later date; and uninhibited by empathic response to the intended victims fear. Sometimes the explanation for violence may be similar to that given by Raskolnikov in Dosteyevsky's Crime and Punishment: that is it is of an experimental nature. It is often a wish to experience a sense of mastery and control over another person. They may also do it to test their predictions about how others would behave in such extreme circumstances.

But what about psychopathic or sociopathic behaviour where does this fall in the Spectrum, with many of the behaviour traits linked to abusive behaviour, psychopaths charm, lie, manipulate and show a complete lack of remorse these are the character traits. Usually people understand social rules, but psychopaths and sociopaths prioritise their own self interest. They see people as merely a means to an end, they lack empathy, they feel no remorse for their actions, lie easily without hesitation and relate to people in a distorted way Psychopaths process information, make decisions and behaviour between the sexes differs as females tend to be less violent than males although they can be just as remorseless and manipulative. Researchers have posited that there are two subtypes of psychopath, the primary type shows distinct neurological deficits and blunting of emotions, whilst the secondary type exhibits more anxiety, substance misuse abuse and other mental health problems. Not all sociopaths or psychopaths are violent but when they are they tend to be cruel and criminally diverse. They repeat their crimes more often than non psychopathic offenders, they are usually more destructive and their offenses are primarily those that involve self gain, such as theft, or selling illegal drugs. Many are predatory being acutely attuned to their own advantage. Psychopaths exist across all cultures and ethnic groups, There are 16 distinct behaviour traits including, irresponsibility, self centeredness, egotistical, superficial charm, dishonesty, manipulation, lack of guilt or remorse, empathy, lack of deep emotional attachments to others; promiscuity, lying, narcissism; impulsive, antisocial behaviour, dishonesty, and reckless risk-taking. Psychopaths have deficits in conceptual reasoning, mental flexibility, and problem solving, but they excel in deception and manipulation. They have a stronger need for others approval, poor self image and will use flirtation and sexual behaviour, feign suicide attempts or pretend to be the victim to get what they want or where they need to be. They will also be attracted to jobs involving power status excitement and money.

There appears to be a link especially between psychopaths and borderline personality disorder (BDP) which is characterised by emotional instability, impulsive behaviour and unstable relationships, or excessive superficial relationships or promiscuity. Borderline psychopathy share neurological and cognitive similarities along with Pathological Demand Avoidance (PDA), which suggests that they all have common dispositional vulnerability.

Psychopaths hope to orchestrate a con, whilst those with BP seek to meet desperate needs, People with BP look for strength and stability in others so they can siphon it, whilst psychopaths attune to vulnerability, and don't fear abandonment the way those with BP often do. Psychopathy, Borderline Personality and Pathological Demand Avoidance at present are separate diagnoses, where there is an overlap, but we are likely to see psychopathic features secondary to abuse or neglect where psychopathic behaviours look like BP might stem from adverse experiences. BP experience high degrees of emotional instability, display cutting or suicidal ideations and they struggle with self image.

Abusers brains particularly those involved in the social process and moral reasoning are related to abnormalities in parts of the prefrontal cortex and the amygdala, abusers have great difficulty working through moral concepts and recognising emotional expressions, their shallow emotions are linked to aggressive reactions and perceived frustrations or provocations, they over focus on reward control and under respond to the threat of punishment where we can also recognise these traits in other personality behavioural traits discussed in this book, science has yet to link or been slow to prove and we hope that in the future researchers will look to the autistic population as there is a lot to be learnt from people with autism and it could be productive research.

Chapter 9

Celebrities on the Spectrum

While being on the spectrum can sometimes create challenges, these famous people with autism have been able to use their unique way of seeing the world to achieve great feats. Some of these famous people with autism may surprise you. You may not have known that some of the best-known stars or some of the world's most fascinating minds are actually on the spectrum. Some famous people on the autism spectrum are high-functioning which means that they can better integrate into society - even if they often see things slightly differently from the rest of their peers.

Others, however, are more strongly affected. One-third of those with autism suffer from an intellectual disability, and about just as many are susceptible to epilepsy.

But autism isn't without its gifts. The unique wiring of the brain often gives people with autism a whole different outlook on the world, letting them see it in ways other people wouldn't even consider. And with that unique perspective can there also be an incredible memory or an unrelenting focus on one's passions.

Perhaps that's how these famous people with autism were able to become successful. Experts have also posited that many of these famous people with autism throughout history may well have gone through most of if not all of their lives unaware that they even had the condition.

But without the unique point of view that autism creates some of the great breakthroughs in human history may never have happened.

Without people to see things a little different our world would simply stay the same. While we are well aware that retrospective diagnosis of Autism is near impossible. Despite the challenges associated with the exact identification of Autism related traits, we would like to think that this chapter would be helpful and inspiring to those who themselves fall somewhere on the Spectrum.

Famous Autistic People in History Include Dan Aykroyd - Comedic Actor, Hans Christian Andersen - Children's Author, Benjamin Banneker - African American almanac author, surveyor, naturalist, and farmer. Benjamin Banneker was an African-American author, surveyor, naturalist, astronomer, inventor, and farmer who lived as a free man in 18th century America. Plenty of contemporary documents refer to Banneker's "unparalleled brilliance" and "odd methods of behaviour," lending credence to the common idea that Banneker had a high-functioning form of autism. He was known to fixate on certain objects, such as a friend's watch, until that fixation ultimately led to an experiment or invention of his own.

Singer Susan Boyle, most people know Susan Boyle as the shy Scottish introvert who sold more than 14 million albums after appearing on Britain's Got Talent. But even more people found Boyle inspiring when she announced she had been diagnosed with Asperger's Syndrome, a diagnosis that Boyle said, felt like "a relief." Boyle is still learning about the autism spectrum and how it affects her, but as long as she keeps singing, people are sure to continue to be inspired by her. Movie Director Tim Burton Is Hollywood director Tim Burton Autistic? His long-time partner, Helena Bonham Carter, seems to think so. At least, she once speculated that he was "possibly autistic" during an interview. While researching an autistic character for a film, Carter claims, she had an "a-ha moment" and realised that much of her research applied to Burton. Said Carter, "Autistic people have application and dedication. You can say something to Tim when he's working and he doesn't hear you. But that quality also makes him a fantastic father; he has an amazing sense of humour and imagination. He sees things other people won't see."

Lewis Carroll - Author of "Alice in Wonderland" There are few historical figures as controversial as Lewis Carroll, the author of the children's classic Alice in Wonderland. While some of his behaviour, such as continuously seeking out the company of young girls, has made some wonder if the university professor was a pedophile, others use the same information to insist that Carroll was actually autistic. After all, Carroll lived in a different time and place, with far different social customs than what we are used to today. He was also known to be a poor communicator, and therefore likely found interacting with children much easier. His difficulty with communication was exacerbated by a severe stammer. Finally, Carroll showed great mathematical ability and even considered himself to be a minor inventor, both common characteristics of those on the spectrum.

Scientist Henry Cavendish is perhaps one of the most important scientists in history. A natural philosopher, chemist, and physicist, Cavendish is perhaps most famous as the discoverer of hydrogen. He is also thought to have been autistic. Besides his weekly meetings at the prestigious Royal Society Club, Cavendish did all he could to avoid company and social calls. Indeed, he was so reclusive, he communicated with his servants in writing, ordered his meals via a note left on the table, and even added a private staircase to the back of his house so as to avoid the housekeeper. He also avoided eye contact and was described by a contemporary as the "coldest and most indifferent of mortals." But he was also brilliant, though it was only after his death that fellow scientists went through his many papers and realized all he had accomplished.

Charles Darwin, Naturalist, Geologist, and Biologist Trinity College professor Michael Fitzgerald, a leading psychiatrist, researched and published a paper concluding that Charles Darwin had Asperger's Syndrome. There are records from Darwin's childhood that state he was a very quiet and isolated child, who avoided interaction with others as much as he could. Like so many others with Asperger's, he sought alternative ways of communicating, such as writing letters. He had fixations with certain topics like chemistry, but was a very visual thinker - all traits of someone on the autism spectrum.

Poet Emily Dickinson, In her book Writers on the Spectrum: How Autism and Asperger's Syndrome have Influenced Literary Writing, academic Julie Brown includes classical poet Emily Dickinson. Brown is part of a large group who believe Dickinson showed plenty of signs of being autistic: she wrote poems that were extremely unconventional for her time period, she was reclusive, she got along best with children, she wore white clothing almost exclusively, and had a fascination with scented flowers, among other things. While Dickinson's biographer, Lyndall Gordon, insists that Dickinson's epilepsy is what made her so reclusive, medical professionals are quick to point out that those with autism have a much higher chance of also having epilepsy.

Physicist Paul Dirac has repeatedly been referred to as one of the most significant and influential physicists of the 20th century. The Cambridge professor greatly contributed to early quantum mechanics and quantum electrodynamics, and even received the Nobel Prize in Physics in 1933. That Nobel, however, was almost refused by Dirac, who was so reclusive that he didn't want the publicity. Such shyness is one of many reasons why a large number of people think Dirac may have had some form of autism. Besides his shyness, they cite his intense focus, extreme literal mindedness, lack of empathy, and his rigid patterns, among other things.

Scientist and Mathematician, Albert Einstein was perhaps the most famous scientist and mathematician in history, Albert Einstein had a number of interesting and possibly telling characteristics. For one, he had trouble socialising, especially as an adult. As a child, he experienced severe speech delays and later echolalia, or the habit of repeating sentences to himself. And of course, there is the fact that Einstein was incredibly technical. Such characteristics have led many experts to conclude that he appeared somewhere on the Autism Spectrum.

Chess Grandmaster Bobby Fischer, World Chess Champion, is said to have had Asperger's Syndrome in addition to paranoid schizophrenia and Obsessive Compulsive Disorder. Fischer was known to be extremely intense, and did not relate well to others thanks to his lack of friendships and poor social abilities. His extreme focus on chess is another sign, as his track record for not being able to cope in an unstructured environment.

Co-founder of the Microsoft Corporation Could Bill Gates, one of the richest men in the world be on the Autistc Spectrum? Quite a few Autism experts seem to think so! While nothing has ever been confirmed regarding whether or not Gates falls on the Autism Spectrum, those who seem to think he is cite things like the distinct rocking motion Gates displays when he concentrates, his shortened and mono toned speech patterns, and his habits of avoiding eye contact on the rare occasion he speaks directly with someone else. These are all common characteristics of those on the Spectrum, and the evidence that Bill Gates may be Autistic is probably quite persuasive.

Temple Grandin the Animal Scientist. There may be no Autistic person alive today more famous than Temple Grandin. The author and Colorado State University professor didn't begin speaking until she was almost four years old, and the doctors who diagnosed her recommended she be institutionalised. Fortunately, her parents did not agree with those doctors. Grandin has gone on to become a leading force in animal sciences, has been named one of TIME's 100 most influential people, and even produced an award-winning biopic about her life. She remains an outspoken advocate in the Autism community, and has been unapologetic about her belief that the "characteristics of Autism can be modified and controlled."

Actress and Environmental Activist Daryl Hannah the beautiful star of films like Splash, Blade Runner, and Steel Magnolias, only came out about her experiences on the Autism Spectrum about five years ago. Since then, Hannah has been nothing but inspirational as she's told the honest truth about her challenges with Asperger's Syndrome. As a child, she rocked herself to self-soothe, and was so shy that once she began acting she refused to give interviews or even attend her own premieres. Though she has mostly learned to control and live with her diagnosis, Hannah has all but left the entertainment industry to focus on environmental issues and other passions.

Thomas Jefferson an early American Politician. This one is probably especially controversial. Those who argue that the third president of the United States fell somewhere on the Autism Spectrum cite the fact that Jefferson was well-known to have been an uncomfortable public speaker and one who could not relate well to others. A number of contemporary documents even reference Jefferson's sensitivity to loud noises and his many strange routines, such as the constant companionship of a pet mockingbird. Despite the evidence, the best we can do when it comes to Jefferson is speculate, as most documents dating from his early life burned down with his childhood home.

Steve Jobs the Former CEO of Apple and those who associate Steve Jobs with Autism admit that it's pure speculation, but they are also quick to point out that that speculation has grown more and more mainstream since the Apple genius's death in 2011. Those who believe Jobs landed somewhere on the Spectrum cite such behavioural quirks as his obsession with perfection, and his unorthodox ways of thinking. His general lack of empathy when dealing with others and his personal relationships were heavily portrayed in the feature film on his life as having many of the Autistic Spectrum traits we have talked about.

James Joyce Author of "Ulysses", Ask any Autism expert about James Joyce, and you'll likely hear them argue that his writing itself is extreme evidence of Joyce possibly being Autistic. After all, his two most famous works, "Ulysses" and "Finnegan's Wake", are brilliant, yet intentionally difficult to read and understand. As Joyce told Harper's Magazine, "The demand that I make of my reader is that he should devote his whole life to reading my work." Some claim that this intentional approach to his work showed Joyce's desire to distance himself from society, a very Autistic thing to do. These same scholars also reference Joyce's youth, during which he was extremely intelligent, but he also suffered from a number of phobias and had trouble keeping friends

Sexologist and Biologist, Alfred Kinsey was a famed sexologist and biologist who founded the Kinsey Institute for Research in Sex, Gender, and Reproduction. As is just about anything in his line of work, Kinsey was extremely controversial. Though the controversy surrounding his work has died down since Kinsey's death, a new controversy has since arisen asking the question, was Kinsey Autistic? Many medical professionals seem to think so. In 1999 an article in the Journal of Autism and Developmental Disorders stated that Kinsey met the criteria for Asperger's Syndrome because of his "qualitative impairment in social interaction," "failure to develop appropriate peer relationships," and "lack of social and emotional reciprocity."

Film Director Stanley Kubrick is most famous as the innovative and exceedingly creative director of films like "A Clockwork Orange," "Dr. Strangelove," and "2001: A Space Odyssey." But could he also have had some form of Autism? The experts are split on this one. Those who argue that Kubrick was indeed Autistic cite the director's reclusive nature and his habit of hoarding animals. He was a chess mastermind, and said to be uncomplimentary and cheap. Still, there are plenty of reports that refute these allegations.

Scientist and Cytogeneticist Barbara McClintock was a famed scientist who made great breakthroughs in the study of chromosomes and how they change during the reproduction process. McClintock has long been thought of as Autistic in some way. She had an extreme fixation on her work and was able to focus for long periods of time. She was also very particular about what she would and would not wear. Notably reclusive and one who went to great lengths to avoid any attention of limelight, McClintock nearly didn't accept the 1983 Nobel Prize in Physiology or Medicine that she was awarded for her excellent and ground breaking work.

Michelangelo Sculptor, Painter, Architect, Poet. Dr. Muhammad Arshad published in the Royal Society of Medicine's Journal of Medical Biography a convincing paper arguing that Michelangelo was almost certainly Autistic. Another leading researcher on the topics, Professor Michael Fitzgerald, agrees. Their evidence: the artist's singular interest in his work, a temper that could change at the drop of a hat, strict routines, and very poor social skills. Such characteristics, all of which were determined through dozens of contemporary notes and letters, are consistent with those with high-functioning Autism.

Classical Composer Wolfgang Amadeus Mozart. As most scholars agree that musical maestro Mozart was somewhere on the Spectrum. Mozart was allegedly extremely sensitive to loud noises, had a notoriously short attention span, and could fly through a cycle of facial expressions within seconds. In one well documented incident, a bored Mozart began doing cartwheels and vaults over tables while meowing loudly like a cat.

Mathematician, Astronomer, and Physicist Sir Isaac Newton with thanks to researchers at Cambridge University, we have a pretty good idea that Isaac Newton had Asperger's Syndrome or something else on the Spectrum. The researchers, who also argued that Albert Einstein was Autistic, mention in their article evidence that Newton isolated himself as much as possible and was notoriously awkward when it came to typical daily conversation. He was not good at keeping friends, and relied strongly upon routines. Lastly, there are a number of reports that suggest that he was often so focused on his work, that he went for days at a time without eating or sleeping as he was obsessive in his work.

Jerry Seinfeld, one of the most popular comedians of all time, has said in multiple interviews that he believes himself to be on the Autism Spectrum. Though he has never been officially diagnosed by a medical professional, Seinfeld has defended his self-diagnosis by citing various social challenges that he has experienced since childhood, as well as his tendency to think literally. While Seinfeld may consider himself to have Asperger's Syndrome, others in the Autism community disagree. In fact, Seinfeld's revelation has been quite controversial, with many feeling that his self-diagnosis has only served to make light of actual issues.

As a child, Satoshi Tajiri, the Creator of Nintendo's Pokémon was fascinated by insects and was even nicknamed "Dr. Bug" by other children. As an adult, Tajiri turned that interest into the world-wide phenomenon that is Pokemon - which itself makes him an inspiration to millions of children (and adults!) around the world. But Satoshi Tajiri is also on the high-functioning end of the Autism Spectrum. Though he confirmed that he does indeed have Asperger's Syndrome, Tajiri does not talk about it in public, choosing instead to let his many accomplishments speak for themselves.

Nikola Tesla the Inventor, who was a major rival of Thomas Edison, reportedly stole many of his best ideas, Nikola Tesla died poor and alone. More recently, Tesla is finally getting the credit he deserves for many of his most genius ideas. It's likely the inventor was also Autistic. According to records of Tesla's time, he suffered from a large number of phobias, was extremely sensitive to light and sound, isolated himself, and was obsessed with the number three.

Judith Gould, the Director of the leading diagnostic centre for Autism in the United Kingdom, insists that it makes perfect sense that Andy Warhol the artist was Autistic. After all, much of the artist's work focuses on repetition, on which those with Autism usually fixate. In interviews, Warhol almost always responded to questions with mono-syllabic answers, possibly evidence that he had the verbal dyslexia that is so common among those on the Spectrum. He reportedly refused to wear anything but a certain kind of green underwear. Still, not everyone agrees that Warhol was Autistic. Those who argue against this posthumous diagnosis suggest that Warhol's different behaviour was calculated in an effort to "enhance a sense of mystery."

The Austrian philosopher Ludwig Wittgenstein is another inspiring historical figure who very likely had Autism. In fact, Wittgenstein's most famous work, "Tractatus Logico-Philosophicus" has been cited again and again as a classical example of the Autistic thought process. Contemporary letters and diary entries reference Wittgenstein's persistent irritation, especially when it came to understanding and dealing with those around him.

Poet Professor Michael Fitzgerald, the same Trinity College professor who recently published a paper asserting that Charles Darwin likely had some form of Autism, claims the same thing about Irish poet William Butler Yeats. Fitzgerald cites Yeats' extreme difficulty in school, where he was bullied for his lack of interest and awkward social behaviour. He also brings up the fact that Yeats pined for years for Maud Gonne, despite her stated disinterest. Still, Yeats' biographer, Oxford professor Roy Foster, rejects Fitzgerald's idea's.

In 1807 the poet George Byron then aged 19 years became known as one of the most sexual adventurers in the world. He was 5ft '8 inches and weighed 14.6 stone, which by today's standards is classed as obese. His weight fluctuated widely throughout his life, characterised by bouts of binging, purging, and starving which we today would recognise as an eating disorder. He is believed to have confided in his confidant Lady Melbourne about that in 1813. Byron's family on both sides had a history of infamy, depression and madness. His maternal grandfather and great grandfather committed suicide; Byron's father was a known womanising gambler; and Byron's mother bullied yet spoiled her only son who also had a disability with a deformed foot. When he was nine years of age Byron was sexually abused by his nursemaid and beaten and bruised. Food became his addiction and it has been estimated that he had over 200 liaisons with prostitutes in a 5 year period, not accounting for the numerous children he fathered and women he had scandalised in sexual affairs. Byron's obsession with measuring his waist and wrists became his trademark to reassure himself when he was not putting weight on. He died in 1824 from a convulsive seizure which was later diagnosed as epilepsy. Perhaps Byron's secret appetite drove Byron's obsession more than his appetite addiction for sex. Perhaps had the words Autism Spectrum been around in the great poets days, he may of understood his behaviours more and been ready to try and do something about them, instead trying to alleviate his pain by indulging in women, he fantasised his pain away by dreaming of becoming a politician or statesman.

Sir Philip Anthony Hopkins CBE is a Welsh film, stage, and television actor and socially introverted Considered to be one of the greatest living actors, Born in 1937 Hopkins is well known for his portrayal of Hannibal Lecter in The Silence of the Lambs, for which he won the Academy Award for Best Actor, and in its sequel Hannibal, and the prequel Red Dragon. In interviews over the past few years Anthony Hopkins admits he was diagnosed with high-end Asperger's syndrome, a neurological condition that affects social interaction. He is, he says himself, very much a loner. 'I don't go to parties, I don't have many friends,' he says. 'But I do like people. I do like to get inside their heads.' He was asked whether he thinks Asperger's has helped him as an actor. He nods his head. 'I definitely look at people differently.

Gary Numan Born Gary Webb in 1958 is a English singer, composer, and musician, has Asperger syndrome, an Autism Spectrum disorder which causes restricted social and communication skills. In a 2001 interview, he said: "Polite conversation has never been one of my strong points. Just recently I actually found out that I'd got a mild form of Asperger's syndrome which basically means I have trouble interacting with people. For years, I couldn't understand why people thought I was arrogant, but now it all makes more sense".

Former boxing promoter Kellie Maloney has revealed she attempted suicide after falling in with the wrong crowd and missing her previous life as a boxing promoter, known previously as the transgender star said she was mixing with the wrong friends which lead to doubts over her transition. The former Celebrity Big Brother and Masterchef star says she does not regret undergoing gender reassignment surgery but fell into a dark place and began having doubts. Whilst as yet there is no clinical research to suggest that Kelly could fit the spectrum criteria she fits into a number of categories on the Spectrum, she has not had any formal diagnosis which could explain her difficulties.

Caitlin Jenner - Originally born William Bruce Jenner; October 28, 1949 is an American television personality and retired Olympic gold medal winning decathlete, probably more best known for being the father of the Kardashian girls. Jenner has six children with three successive wives, Chrystie Crownover, Linda Thompson, and Kris Jenner and he has since 2007 appeared on the reality television series Keeping Up with the Kardashians with Kris, their daughters Kendall and Kylie Jenner, and Kris's other children Kourtney, Kim, Khloé, and Rob Kardashian.

Jenner came out as a trans woman, saying that she had dealt with gender dysphoria since her youth and that, "for all intents and purposes, I'm a woman." Jenner cross dressed for many years and took hormone replacement therapy but stopped after her romance with Kris Kardashian became more serious, leading to marriage in 1991. Assigned male at birth, Caitlyn Jenner publicly came out as a trans woman in April 2015. Her new name was publicly announced in July of that year, with her name and gender being legally changed the following September. From 2015 to 2016, Jenner starred in the reality television series I Am Cait, which focused on her gender transition. In January 2017, she underwent sex reassignment surgery. Because of her reality TV fame Jenner has been called the most famous transgender woman in the world. Jenner similarly as Maloney may of attributed their physical abilities to ADHD but no formal research has been identified as yet.

Singer Elton John a former alcoholic drug user binge eater shop a holic obsessive collector musician has a number of impulsive personality traits going on and freely admits to them. Whilst Singer songwriters, Lionel Richie, Gabrielle Emanuel and Toyah Wilcox have openly admitted being dyslexic to the British Media.

Businessman and former Dragons' Den star Theo Paphitis has credited dyslexia for his success. The disorder, which affects reading, writing and spelling, forced him to find solutions. "It's fair to say that I wasn't a model pupil at school, and the teachers weren't interested as they thought I was thick. I wasn't. I was actually dyslexic and although it made school harder, it also gave me the tools to create alternative solutions. However, I did always have my eye on making money and working in business, particularly as I came from a background where we had very little. There have been many factors, but I suspect I wouldn't be where I was today without being dyslexic. When people ask whether I wish I didn't have dyslexia, I think... I haven't done that badly with it! Dyslexia has made me create a whole new world for myself in finding alternative solutions from the norm for processing and analysing information, particularly in business. I know I'm not alone here. Buckets full of hard work, passion and a competitive nature have all certainly helped too". As far as we are aware Theo does not have a formal dyslexia diagnosis.

Business Woman and former Spice Girl Singer Victoria Beckham has described herself as a self-diagnosed dyslexic. Victoria said none of her four children was especially academic, adding that 'dyslexia doesn't run in our family, it gallops', Limiting problems with reading, writing and spelling. Singer songwriter Toyah Wilcox has a diagnosis of dyslexia and struggled tremendously as a child. Mathematician TV Personality Carol Vorhdman has son Cameron who has very severe dyslexia. You could also apportion Carols extreme mathematical ability to being on the spectrum due to her amazing mathematical abilities.

As yet there is no defined scientific link between dyslexia, dyspraxia, dyscalculia and other learning difficulties of number, word blindness or clumsiness. However they all seem to contribute and play a significant part on the spectrum where the individuals displaying them also display other high flying, autistic traits.

Taking this a generation further Sylvester Stallone's son, Seargeoh (born 1979), was diagnosed with autism at age three. In an interview from the early 1980s, Stallone said, "You can't force him into your world. I sort of go along with whatever he is doing." Quarter back Dan Marino's son, Michael (born 1988), was diagnosed with autism when he was two years old. Marino says, "It's extremely important that people recognize that with the right proper care, and the proper therapies, that kids can definitely get better and have a great life." Singer Toni Braxton's son, Diezel (born 2003), was diagnosed with autism in 2006. For some time, Braxton believed that her son's Autism was God's way of punishing her for having an abortion in 2001.She later said, "When my youngest son was diagnosed with autism I feared that I was being punished for my earlier actions. I have since realized that my son is special and learns in a different way."

TV host Jenny McCarthy's son, Evan (born 2002), was diagnosed with autism in 2005. McCarthy believes that the disorder was caused by vaccination Actor and dancer John Travolta and Kelly Preston's son, Jett (born 1992), had autism and suffered from seizures. Sadly, Jett passed away after having a seizure while the family was on vacation in the Bahamas in 2009. Model and reality star Katie Price's son, Harvey was born in 2002 with the genetic disorder Prader-Willi syndrome. This condition leaves people feeling constantly hungry and can lead to diabetes and obesity. It also affects intellectual and behavioural development. Children who are diagnosed with AS are characterised by social difficulties that lie along the autism spectrum disorder (ASD) continuum. Certain gene abnormalities leading to PWS and Angelman syndrome lie within genetic regions that are also thought to be associated with Autism Spectrum disorder. Actress Emma Noble, daughter in law of the former Prime Minister John Major, says of her son Harry, now aged 19 "I could not live without him and I would not want him any other way," she says.

Boyzone singer Keith Duffy's daughter 18 year old daughter, Mia, has Autism. In a natural human response, the couple wondered if they were somehow at fault. "My wife never smoked or drank when pregnant, she's very healthy but she blamed herself and what she could have done differently when she was pregnant". TV Presenter Actress and model Melanie Syke's son Valentino was diagnosed with autism in 2012. He is an amazing little boy and he has changed my life. I want everybody to know that if you have a diagnosis of autism today, there is so much you can do with your child. It is miraculous.'

Actress Sally Phillip's eldest son, 14 year old Ollie, has Downs Syndrome. An increasing number of children with Down syndrome are being diagnosed as also having autism or autistic spectrum disorder (ASD). Research is exploring the prevalence and the characteristics of autism and autistic spectrum disorders in people with Down syndrome, and informing more reliable diagnosis. More research is needed to better understand these dual diagnoses.

Christine and Paddy McGuiness, the model and comedian opened up about being parents to three autistic children, five-year-old twins Penelope and Leo and two-year-old Felicity. Christine said that as a way to help her children feel less overwhelmed by day to day activities, she has created a visual calendar and takes pictures of the places they are going to visit so they know when to expect.

Scott Davies was, at one point, training with Reading's first team in the Premier League. By his late twenties, he had lost over £200,000 to gambling, was left without a club contract, and was having suicidal thoughts. Over that period, he dropped down through the Championship, League Two into the Southern League Premier Division. Now aged 30, he hasn't put a bet on since 2015, and he is using his experience of addiction to help other athletes who may be struggling with gambling-related issues.

Michael Phelps, hailed as the greatest Olympian American swimmer ever, has attention deficit hyperactivity disorder, along with British gymnast Louis Smith, who helped win the first British men's gymnastics team medal for a century.

But Ashley McKenzie's story is perhaps most dramatic of all. Expelled from three schools and placed in a psychiatric unit aged 11 because his mother was unable to cope, McKenzie also served time in a young offenders' institute. He credits judo with saving him from prison. McKenzie served three bans from judo for drinking and fighting, and on the last night of the Team GB training camp before the Olympics, he went out to celebrate his 23rd birthday and told a stranger at a bar: "I'm gonna smash your face in." His ADHD may bequeath him energy but his sporting career is actually a hindrance to tackling his condition: he cannot take the medication he needs to treat his

ADHD because it contains substances banned by the sporting authorities - hence his struggle to control his behaviour and the stigma that surrounds the issue.

Louis Smith in 2008 took bronze and silver in gymnastic at the Olympics in 2008. Former BBC Strictly Dancing Winner believes his ADHD helped contribute to his Olympic success. ADHD might actually have positive effects on sports performance, and we need to look more at studies in this area, researchers are just scratching the surface on understanding the unique effects of ADHD on athletes. Chart topping singer songwriter Gabrielle suffered from anxiety and depression having also recently discovered her symptoms were also caused by having ADHD. Justin Timberlake confesses to ADHD and OCD and ADD. Actress Paris Hilton in an interview with Larry King admitted to ADD and has been on medication since she was a child. Singer Solange Knowles sister of Beyonce has an ADHD diagnosis.

Harry Houdini ninety three years on from his death, was a shameless narcissist by todays standards, ruthless in his pursuit and desire for fame and relentless in his quest for acknowledgement, to make his name a household word. He had an unpleasant personality too by all accounts, under his real name Ehrich Weiss he was described as manipulative, divisive and a complicated figure who was obsessed with his own legend, a habitual liar who squared up to anyone who challenged him, hidden behind the smoke and mirrors that the great escapologist created for himself.

Lastly we would like mention the portrayal of personality types in modern literature, who you may consider to have mental affiliations take Winnie The Poo who could be seen to have an eating disorder, Piglet displays anxiety disorder, Tigger ADHD, Rabbit OCD, Eeaor major depression, Kanga social anxiety as an over protective mother and the Owl narcissistic personality disorder. Perhaps the most surprising disorder suffer of all is Christopher Robin schizophrenia. That is until you realise all his 'friends' and actually stuffed toys. It is likely that by creating these characters in his head, they are representing feelings that he actually experiences him Perhaps we could take these examples further looking at Snow White and the Seven Dwarfs the Wombles and other characters.

The lists of people with AS behavioural are by no means exhausted, there are many more celebrities athletes and high profile personalities on the Spectrum just as there are of the general public who openly discuss or attribute their abilities to being on the Spectrum. For example many comedians comic timing could be down to ADHD and the high functioning side of (ASD) being able to openly communicate with ease. In the case of well known comedian Lee Mack, you will see on TV if you watch closely enough he has a form of facial ticks or mild Tourette's in the way he blinks his eyes, we do not know if Lee Mack is even aware of his facial expressions let alone if he would even consider himself to have traits or undergo a diagnosis. Comedian Jess Thom is best known for being a Tourettes hero. With her alter ego increasing awareness of the condition as a disabled activist she sees her Tourettes as her source of creativity.

Many celebrities may have siblings or other family members with similar or different traits as discussed. One thing in all of this seems to be is that Spectrum conditions do not seem to be going away, and as science advances further won't be pushed to the side lines. As the number of cases in our family members increases so does our continual questioning arises.

Chapter 10

Love and Relationships on the Spectrum

Although some people on the Autism spectrum enjoy fulfilling relationships, there are others for whom emotional attachment can be
difficult and this may affect intimate relationships, family relationships
and friendships. We are presenting the views of some of the people
on the Spectrum and, in some cases, their partners.

Some people in the counselling setting in long-term relationships,
married or living together, sometimes with children, talked about positive and difficult aspects of their relationships with people on the
Spectrum. One woman thought that people with Autism like traits like
to enter into relationships with people who are very caring and "they
pick someone who compensates for what they lack". This can be best
described in many aspects of emotions and traits that are Autism related. A few partners said their husbands/partners were very focused
on them when they first met which they thought might be a characteristic of Autistic Spectrum Condition. For example; Obsessive behaviour. "He fell for me and he wanted me and nothing was going to
stop him, he was so kind and thoughtful and loving and giving when
we were courting but it changed the moment we were married. "It is
definitely something you have to work at".

Some couples, said they worked hard at their relationship and supported each other, they enjoyed the familiarity and regularity of knowing
each other. "I don't play social games". Some people were single but
hoped to have a relationship at some point. Others were single after
relationships had not worked and they had decided they were better as
friends. Some Aspies have had such bad negative experiences that they

have shied away from dating altogether, they have given up and prefer to live alone possibly because they have found the sensitiveness and hurt too much to bear when a relationship breaks down. They find themselves unable to socially communicate, find intimacy and touch too invasive or intrusive and end up isolated and alone. Many prefer their own company, as to give of themselves to someone else is too emotionally draining and exhausting and find comfort doing just for themselves is enough for them to cope with day to day.

A couple of people talked about the intense emotional difficulties past relationships had caused them which had led to a form of breakdown. Jess said he was not sure he wants to tolerate the level of pain he experienced after breaking up with his partner. John said that all the girls he had been involved with had "cleared off and married someone else" and he always thought it was because he wasn't really "husband material".

Other people also talked about wanting a relationship but finding the social interaction involved in trying to begin a relationship too difficult. This was partly to do with communication difficulties but also to do with a desire to talk about specific interests that may not be shared. One man said that this was an area where he would like some training or support. Many successful Aspie relationships are down to shared interests, hobbies and job specialisms.

Many Aspies also don't conform to dating morals or codes of conduct. For example they will show little or no emotion and will date multiple partners at once, or have an affair, not taking their partner's feelings into account, possess little or no boundaries respect for their partner or put their own needs first and foremost above and beyond their partner's needs. Some Aspies become the usually more vulnerable ones in the relationship whose needs are being put on hold whilst they maintain a relationship more often than not with a controlling more dominant partner.

Daniel found living away from his parents' house difficult; "I don't know why, I just felt uncomfortable. I didn't quite know what it was but it was some need for me to be at home. I just feel safer at home". Some Aspies thrive on familiarity. Another woman said she was asexual and while she had tried relationships in the past, because she thought she ought to, she had realised that she had no sexual desire and was happy on her own. Some women talked about feeling vulnerable and not being very good at judging characters. Two women were divorced after being in abusive relationships, one of the women had had a few abusive relationships before deciding to remain single and bring up her children alone.

From a partner's perspective, some partners of people on the spectrum had difficult lives because their partners often couldn't understand how they felt about things or didn't want to talk things through with them or make joint decisions. Some partners found it difficult to cope with their partners' special interests as some felt isolated and depressed. One woman had been taking sleeping tablets because her husband's behaviour had so distressed her over the years it caused her to feel both depressed because of her lack of sleep and anxious when she was around him. Life became much more difficult when her husband retired because she had "the full volume of his personality and controlling behaviour". Romantic relationships can be complicated and frustrating for a lot of people, on the Autistic Spectrum. One of the main reasons behind this is that those on the spectrum will most likely experience major difficulties with understanding and expressing emotions, especially romantically. Another woman's perspective - I have been diagnosed with high functioning autism, also labelled as Asperger's. I hate labels with a passion, so, I very rarely tell people about this diagnosis. However, in not telling people, it has caused numerous problems as others have failed to understand me properly, and I them. Love, affection and communication can be puzzling for everyone, on the spectrum, more so, it can feel impossible.

For some Aspie's hugging can feel claustrophobic, or unwanted touch. Invasion of their personal space can feel overwhelming or we may find that hugs and cuddles are not very often forthcoming. It is not that cuddles are not welcome, but they have to be given at a time where the person feels comfortable and at ease to give or receive them. If they are in the frame of mind to snuggle, they may never want to let you go.

Some Aspies find it hard communicating, loving words may not feel natural or their timing maybe highly inappropriate. A person on the Spectrum may not understand why the words have to be spoken as actions speak stronger than words. If they have told you they loved you once, they may not see the need to continually repeat it, instead thinking that, of course, you must know as they would tell you if something had changed and they really would!

Some Aspies are highly sensitive to touch and smell and find the intimacy part of relationships and sexual contact too overwhelming. You will probably notice very quickly they have very tender hearts, they may take things you say literally and become hurt over jokey behaviour or innocent comments. Issues surrounding breaking trust and loyalty can be deal breakers. They may be offended easily and also become upset or emotional very quickly about things that may seem trivial or not as upsetting to anyone else.

The myth surrounding Autism, that it meant people had no empathy, is not true. We are more likely have much higher empathy as we feel things for others as though we were experiencing it ourselves, that is if we have had that experience. Some Aspies find it hard to relate to experiences they have yet to experience themselves. If an animal or person is in danger, they will only be able to imagine how they would feel in that situation and not from the other person's perception. This means we will suffer the pain similarly. Whatever the emotion, we will feel it deeply. Comforting words and gentle actions at these times will work wonders in easing pain.

Social situations may be deliberately avoided. You may find that any excuse will be made not to attend family, friends or work social events. You can accept this and understand that these gatherings will cause high anxiety levels, or you can take a few steps to encourage attendance by making the experience a little less stressful. Just by understanding that socialising causes anxiety, can help the person to feel more relaxed immediately; even include a mini debrief of what to expect can be helpful. Small talk is not a speciality, often some Aspies struggle. However, bring up a subject close to your heart and you will find that it is almost impossible to draw the conversation to a close. It can appear a selfish trait. However, it is easier to try to accept that it will be a struggle for you to hold their concentration when discussing things that do not capture their attention.

You may find that Aspie talk almost one-sidedly when it is something we are passionate about. Allow them to talk, but a gentle reminder that a conversation is a two-way thing will also be beneficial. It's a reminder Aspies need to listen more too. Facts, figures, the universe, are all chosen specialisms; these things and more will capture an Aspies attention. Fiction or the latest gossip about other people's private lives will very likely fall on deaf ears. Dates may not be significant, birthdays, anniversaries or other important events are over looked or forgotten, for someone on the Spectrum they may not understand the importance placed on particular dates. If they want to buy you a gift, they will buy you one; they may not feel the need to buy or celebrate just because a date specifies that they should.

You will probably find Aspies will be brutally honest. We will probably say what we think, exactly how we feel and be unfaltering loyal. And we will expect the same in return. Game playing and manipulation will not be our strongest points, purely, because we won't understand them, unless you fall on the part of the spectrum where your personality is narcissistic or borderline then you will have less self awareness of your impact on others, your blindspot means that you will put your needs first at all costs to the detriment of your partner or you may have sociopathic tendencies in love. Aspies if we have something to say, will say it and often be entirely bewildered if we have spoken out of turn.

We Aspies like consistency, changing plans becomes bewildering and confusing to someone on the Spectrum. We will have been thinking about and planning for an event in our minds long before it happens.

Then, when things change, we may find it difficult to cope with the sudden plan change. For some Aspies who cope well with change, just break the changes gently and offer up similar options, if possible. Otherwise, we find its best to just try to be patient and calm and understand that a simple plan change can feel like dramatic and major changes to someone who has Autism. Most Aspies would naturally assume being faithful or having a monogamous relationship would be part of the considered norm. Afterall we thrive on routine and regularity. However romantic and sexual relationships are changing before our eyes and so are the power shifts between men and women as up to 40% of women now earn more than their husbands, and with this gain in social and economic power they are also becoming sexually independent. However as monogamy was once an important considered factor, affairs are becoming gender equal too, especially if you take into account blind spot thinking, personality disorders, self centeredness, and addiction. As more women than men are having affairs today, due to the lack of economic restraints of women being the home maker, their earning power has increased along with their confidence, at street level a number of forces inside and outside relationships are shaping the current state of affairs. Both men and women do cheat because they can, they have more opportunities too and many don't intend to leave their marriages, affairs extra marital flings something for oneself, a moment of pleasure cheating to feel alive, to expand oneself, to risk it all especially in a culture that values narcissism.

Adultery happens across every culture even where you can have your head chopped off for it. Adultery is the clandestine companion of monogamy, the exact opposite end of the spectrum scale, and since prehistory it has been an inherent part of human mating as some Aspies become curious about alternatives. Many people may consider infidelity as sex addiction, they are mainly rebellion, aliveness, freedom, sex and desire, a hunger for awakening and antidote to deadness. Some borderline personalities behaviour is promiscuous to fill the empty void of nothingness, or they develop masochistic tendencies in order to feel. Affairs magnify the difference between being loved and being wanted. So whether the Aspie in your life has been faithful or not, whether it can be pinned or not down to a chink in their personality, or attributed to a specific behavioural trait, our partners do not belong to us they are only on loan with an option to renew.

Most Aspies have a heightened sensory perception to lights, noises, temperatures and numerous other variables will affect the mood of someone with Autism. Keep noise and lighting soft and gentle, anything harsh may cause slight anxieties. Things like the cinema, supermarkets and nightclubs can all feel traumatic to the ears and eyes and can result in tempered frustrations and irritable behaviours. If Aspies need to leave, understand. It is not that they are being awkward, it is just these environments can feel extremely volatile and the effects on them can last for hours afterwards.

Meltdowns, however big or small, will likely take place from time to time when in a relationship with someone on the Spectrum. The way someone handles having a meltdown will differentiate person to person. Meltdowns usually appear after a build up of tension, frustration or a reaction to the environment around them. Meltdowns can be purely emotional or can also be anger fuelled tantrums and majorly traumatic. They seem to accelerate quickly and can come from nowhere.

The most loving thing you can do at this time is to soothe, and calm them. Aspies need to know they are safe, engaging in any kind of argument or confrontation at this time will very likely be futile. Talking things through with your partner when things are calm and discover mutually agreeable ways of dealing with meltdowns so you can be more prepared for next time so by being supportive and caring will bond and build trust between you both, fuelling things with provocative behaviour in return will likely bring resentments. The easiest way to love someone on the Spectrum is by learning to accept them for who they are, trying to change them will not be possible. Even if they do change slightly they will be extremely unhappy on the inside and will be living a life that does not feel natural to them.

People with Autism prefer partners on the spectrum, and often the deficits in one partner can be over compensated by the other partner. If one partner is more socially active than there partner the less socially active one lives their life through the active one. Many successful Aspie partnerships are ones where mirroring behaviours occur between the two, mirroring is the behaviour in which one person subconsciously imitates the gesture, speech pattern, or attitude of another. Mirroring often occurs in social situations, particularly in the company of close friends or family. Mirroring is the subconscious replication of another person's nonverbal signals.

Most Aspies form relationships, friendships and love by association. Our earliest childhood attachments, go on to form our relationships with others in the future. For example one theorist, Bowlby, suggests that attachment takes place during a critical period. It is suggested that if a child does not form an attachment before the critical period (2.5 years) attachment will not occur. (Bowlby later proposed a sensitive period of up to 5 years.) His theories in brief provide a template for future attachments and human relationships.

When we watch the behavioural patterns that characterise this relationship with our main care provider, four types of attachment are seen, these are secure, avoidant, ambivalent, and disorganised. For example if you grew up in care from an early age, or your parent was an addict, its more likely that you will have a disorganised attachment to other people style. If both parents were in a secure relationship and you had a very loving secure up bringing, its more than probable you form secure bonding relationships with others. If your parents were rather avoidant or ambivalent in your care, for example they put their own needs first, showed sociopathic, bi polar, narcissistic tendencies, or other personality disorder behavioural traits, you may have ambivalent or avoidant attachment styles to others.

The main idea of attachment theory is that the caregiver provides the baby with a safe and secure base from which to explore the world. The baby knows that it is safe to venture out and explore the world, and that the caregiver will always be there to come back to for comfort in times of stress and discomfort, our attachment styles are formed based upon our earliest relationships with the caregiver and their relationship to us. If we experienced ambivalent and avoidant caregiving for example, our care giver may have had undiagnosed bi polar disorder we will experience problems forming attachments with our lovers and pier circle groups as our friends may be displaying similar behavioural traits, highs and lows in their personality or on and off irregular patterns.

As we grow older and we realise that we may have had a secure or dysfunctional upbringing we may also realise that we may be repeating these behaviours in our closest friendships and relationships, we become pathological in trying to make these relationships work, not realising that we may be the root cause of our own problems based on our attachment styles. Breaking cyclical patterns of negative destructive behaviour is hard especially for us Aspies who thrive on routine, familiarity and regularity. So next time a relationship, friendship or love partnership is not feeling quiet right for you, ask yourself the question and look at the person's characteristics and behavioural traits and see if you can see any similarities to your own up bringing.

Forget the proverb 'opposites attract:' A massive Swedish study suggested that men and women who have a psychiatric condition such as Autism, schizophrenia or attention deficit hyperactivity disorder (ADHD) tend to pair up with people who share their diagnosis. This non random mating pattern, described 24 February in JAMA Psychiatry, may help to explain why these psychiatric conditions often run in families, says lead investigator David Mataix-Cols, professor of clinical neuroscience at the Karolinska Institute in Stockholm, Sweden.

Partners who have different diagnoses may have children with an increased risk of both conditions. For example, a 2005 study found that men and women with autism-like trait symptoms tend to partner and have children who have even more of these symptoms. This has enormous implications for understanding the genetic structure of conditions and how they're transmitted across generations. The sample study included more than 26,000 people with autism, 60,000 with attention deficit hyperactivity disorder (ADHD) and 70,000 with schizophrenia. (Other psychiatric conditions include bipolar disorder, anorexia nervosa and generalised anxiety disorder.) The study used marriage records or birth certificates to identify opposite-sex partners for each individual and the National Patient Register revealed whether these partners had any psychiatric diagnoses. The researchers found that people with each of the psychiatric conditions are more likely than their matched controls to couple with someone who has the same diagnosis. This pattern is more apparent among couples with autism, ADHD or schizophrenia than in those with any of the other conditions. However non random mating does occur across different conditions, too, although people with different diagnoses are slightly less likely to pair up than those with the same condition. Overall, people with psychiatric conditions are about three times more likely to pick a partner who also has a psychiatric diagnosis.

By contrast, non random mating patterns are weaker among people with non psychiatric conditions. However you can also have a shared delusional psychosis, where one sick individual can alter a healthy persons behaviour, which using the mirroring behaviour as mentioned earlier in the chapter can be a result. For example people with Autism, attention deficit, hyperactivity disorder (ADHD), or schizophrenia tend to be attracted with others who also have a psychiatric condition, and some individuals do not find a partner at all - this is our genetic puzzle as It turns out the science behind love is both simpler and more complex than we might think. What we do know, however, is that much of love can be explained by chemistry. So, if there's really a "formula" for love, what is it, and what does it mean?

Often described as a total eclipse of the brain, think of the last time you ran into someone you find attractive. You may have stammered, your palms may have sweated; your heart started thumping, your stomach felt queezy or strange, you may have said something incredibly unintelligent and tripped spectacularly while trying to saunter away. It's no surprise that, for centuries, people thought love and most other emotions, for that matter arose from the heart. As it turns out, love is all about the brain which, in turn, makes the rest of your body go haywire. So can that mean that as well as Autism originating there, love and who we are attracted to could be considered autistic attraction and a trait too?

'Opposites who attract' the concept appears to be related to Coulombs law of physics (1785). The electrical forces between positive (+) and negative (-) is stronger the closer the two move towards each other in nature, and it can also be true in relationships. So whilst opposites attract, so do dysfunctions and mental disorders which naturally seem drawn to each other in a way that that they either compliment or repel one another. The soul attracts that which it secretly harbours that which it loves and also what it fears. So the very thing which it loves and also what it fears you may have the strongest attraction to. For example, Magnetic attraction - introvert/extrovert, hyperactive/ unhurried and sensitive/stoic. Like finds like for example a passive aggressive is attracted to another passive aggressive. OCD appreciates and values another person with similar behaviours and the two can feed off each other, another clear example of this is a borderline personality with a narcissistic person as they both have problems experiencing self awareness and emotion or anxiety or panic attacks are best understood by others who suffer from the same.

Dysfunctions that match are addicts/co-dependents, in order for an addict to thrive they need someone who will enable the addiction. Borderline personality/ dependent personality, the dependent personality will not leave the relationship. The same applies to a bi polar personality and an empath personality, the empath will be sensitive to the emotions of the bi polar personality to maintain the relationship at all costs to the empath. Aggression/suppression - the suppressor admires the aggressor's ability to let go of their anger.

Dysfunctions also include in Parental attraction - a person enters into a relationship with a person because of strong similarities with the parent they most adore, whilst it might be favourable initially, sexual attraction often diminishes when the realisation becomes more apparent. Dysfunctions can occur when you marry the least favourite parent, by contrast some enter into a relationship with a person very similar to the parent they lest liked as a subconscious attempt to heal the broken relationship. Or it can be trauma re hashed – when the trauma has not be dealt with properly. People will often place themselves in similar places of vulnerability for example Abusers and the abused - this is clearly demonstrated when one person finishes with one abusive relationship to enter into another. Until the reason for the tolerance of the abuse is addressed a person will continue to repeat the same abusive pattern. One very good way for releasing this pain is to write a farewell letter to your love affair be it addiction, abusive behaviour or a dysfunctional attachment, you can then fill yourself up spiritually from the gap of the loss.

According to a team of scientists, each category is characterised by its own set of hormones stemming from the brain. Love can be distilled into three categories: lust, attraction, and attachment. Though there are overlaps and subtleties to each, each type is characterised by its own set of hormones. Testosterone and estrogen drive lust; dopamine, norepinephrine, and serotonin create attraction; and oxytocin and vasopressin mediate attachment. Lust is driven by the desire for sexual gratification. The evolutionary basis for this stems from our need to reproduce, a need shared among all living things. Through reproduction, organisms pass on their genes, and thus contribute to the perpetuation of their species. The hypothalamus of the brain plays a big role in this, stimulating the production of the sex hormones testosterone and estrogen from the testes and ovaries.

While these chemicals are often stereotyped as being "male" and "female," respectively, both play a role in men and women. As it turns out, testosterone increases libido in just about everyone. The effects are less pronounced with estrogen, but some women report being more sexually motivated around the time they ovulate, when estrogen levels are highest. The testes and ovaries secrete the sex hormones testosterone and estrogen, driving sexual desire. Dopamine, oxytocin, and vasopressin are all made in the hypothalamus, a region of the brain that controls many vital functions as well as emotion. Several of the regions of the brain that affect love, lust and attraction shut off the prefrontal cortex of the brain, which includes rational behaviour, also the same part of the brain that deals with the executive functioning side of the brain, Many people with Autism have difficulty with executive functioning. They may have trouble with certain skills like planning, staying organised, sequencing information, and self regulating emotions. Some people pay attention to minor details, but have trouble seeing how these details fit into a bigger picture.

Meanwhile, attraction seems to be a distinct, though closely related, phenomenon. While we can certainly lust for someone we are attracted to, and vice versa, one can happen without the other. Attraction involves the brain pathways that control "reward" behaviours, which partly explains why the first few weeks or months of a relationship can be so exhilarating and even all consuming, also known as the honeymoon period.

Dopamine, produced by the hypothalamus, is a particularly well publicised player in the brain's reward pathway it's released when we do things that feel good to us. In this case, these things include spending time with loved ones and having sex. High levels of dopamine and a related hormone, norepinephrine, are released during attraction. These chemicals make us giddy, energetic, and euphoric, even leading to decreased appetite and insomnia which means you actually can be so "in love" that you can't eat and can't sleep. In fact, norepinephrine, also known as noradrenalin, may sound familiar because it plays a large role in the fight or flight response, which kicks into high gear when we're stressed and keeps us alert. Brain scans of people in love have actually shown that the primary "reward" centres of the brain, ignite like crazy when people are shown a photo of someone they are intensely attracted to, compared to when they are shown someone they feel neutral towards (like an old school acquaintance).

Attraction seems to lead to a reduction in serotonin, a hormone that's known to be involved in appetite and mood. Interestingly, people who suffer from obsessive compulsive disorder also have low levels of serotonin, leading scientists to speculate that this is what underlies the overpowering infatuation that characterises the beginning stages of love.

However, attachment style is the predominant factor in long term relationships. While lust and attraction are pretty much exclusive to romantic entanglements, attachment mediates friendships, parent infant bonding, social cordiality, and many other intimacies as well. The two primary hormones here appear to be oxytocin and vasopressin. Oxytocin is often nicknamed "cuddle hormone" for this reason. Like dopamine, oxytocin is produced by the hypothalamus and released in large quantities during sex, breastfeeding, and childbirth. This may seem like a very strange assortment of activities, not all of which are necessarily enjoyable, but the common factor here is that all of these events are precursors to bonding. It also makes it pretty clear why having separate areas for attachment, lust, and attraction is important: we are attached to our immediate family, but those other emotions have no business there let's just say people who have muddled this up (our earliest primary care givers) don't have the best track record in romantic attachments.

This can on the face of it paint quite the rosy picture of love: hormones are released, making us feel good, rewarded, and close to our romantic partners. However love is often accompanied by jealousy, erratic behaviour, anger and irrationality, along with a host of other less than positive emotions and moods. It seems that our friendly cohort of hormones is also responsible for the downsides of love too.

Dopamine, for instance, is the hormone responsible for the vast majority of the brain's reward pathway, that means controlling both the good and the bad. We experience surges of dopamine for our virtues and our vices. In fact, the dopamine pathway is particularly well studied when it comes to addiction. The same regions that light up when we're feeling attraction light up when drug addicts take cocaine and when we binge for example on food or eating sweet things. For example, cocaine maintains dopamine signalling for much longer than usual, leading to a temporary "high." In a way, attraction is much like an addiction to another human being. Similarly, the same brain regions light up when we become addicted to material goods as when we become emotionally dependent on our partners. Addicts going into withdrawal are not unlike love struck people craving the company of someone they cannot see.

Dopamine, which runs the reward pathways in our brain, is great in moderate doses, helping us enjoy food, exciting events, and relationships. However, we can push the dopamine pathway too far when we become addicted to food or drugs. Similarly, too much dopamine in a relationship can underlie unhealthy emotional dependence on our partners, and while healthy levels of oxytocin help us bond and feel warm and fuzzy towards our companions, elevated oxytocin can also fuel prejudice as too much of a good thing can be bad. Recent studies of party drugs such as MDMA and GHB suggest that oxytocin may be the hormone behind the feel good, sociable effects these chemicals produce. These positive feelings are taken to an extreme in this case, causing the user to dissociate from his or her environment and act wildly and recklessly.

Furthermore, oxytocin's role as a "bonding" hormone appears to help reinforce the positive feelings we already feel towards the people we love. That is, as we become more attached to our families, friends, and significant others, oxytocin is working in the background, reminding us why we like these people and increasing our affection for them. While this may be a good things for monogamy, such associations are not always positive. For example, oxytocin has also been suggested to play a role in ethnocentrism, increasing our love for people in our already established cultural groups and making those unlike us seem more foreign. Thus, like dopamine, oxytocin can be a bit of a double edged sword.

What would love be without embarrassment? Sexual arousal (but not necessarily attachment) appears to turn off regions in our brain that regulate critical thinking, self awareness, and rational behaviour, including parts of the prefrontal cortex. In short, love makes us dumb. Have you ever done something when you were in love that you later regretted? Maybe not. I'd ask a certain star crossed Shakespearean couple, but it's a little late for them. Lastly I would like to refer back to mirroring behaviour that we Aspies can do as individuals, for those that have been cheated on, more often than not, but not in every case, they go onto find a new partner and replicate the behaviour that was done to them and cheat on their current partner. This is not ideal behaviour but unless there is a level of self awareness that we talk about, mirroring behaviours in human relationships of all kinds is insurmountable, as often the victim can become perpetrator.

What about what we hear about sex cults with sociopathic leaders, how do people end up being brainwashed into this type of existence, and why don't people walk away from these types of exploitive relationships? What seems to resonate most is the fact that they are a community of like minded humanitarians who want to change the world, often with their own personal insecurities and with something they want to prove to the world.

Lots of people in their late teens and early 20's are searching for a purpose but don't necessarily join cults, however a lot of cults prey on vulnerable people. It's a very normal human thing to want a community, belonging and meaning especially to most Aspies, especially when they don't seem to fit in with their piers. Usually the offer of being some sort leader is a huge promise, a confidence boost to an Aspie whose confidence is already shaky for being different - along with the enticement of personal development, and as the cult develops it strips away any self esteem a person has and then build up your confidence within the cults own regime where an Aspie is made to feel safe. This it's where the most damage can be done as Aspies then become exploitable and extremely vulnerable to a sociopath with little or no emotion as to how others may be feeling.

In relationships, the basics of undue influence, and why individuals on the autism spectrum are uniquely susceptible to it will remain a question still to be answered in more depth however understanding the difference between healthy and unhealthy influence plays an important part in society education. Undue influence is not just an issue for religious cults; it is used by political cults, abusive individuals, trafficking rings, and terrorist groups to recruit, indoctrinate, and maintain control over individuals. Sexual offenders bombard their victims with many many text messages as they want their needs met, it's about their self centeredness unable to gage the effect that this is having on their victims. Voyeuristic sexual tendencies again see no wrong in their actions only satisfying their own needs.

In short, there is sort of a "formula" for love or relationships. However, it's a work in progress, love doesn't care about age, gender, disability, your quirks or deepest flaws; so who ever you fall in love with enjoy it for what it is. There are many questions left unanswered as we've realised by now, it's not just the hormone side of the equation that's complicated. Love and relationships can be both the best and worst thing for you, it can be the thing that gets us up in the morning, or what makes us never want to wake up again. I'm not sure we could define "love" for you if we kept you here for another ten thousand pages. In the end, everyone is capable of defining love and relationships for themselves for better or for worse. If it's all hormones, maybe each of us can have "chemistry" with just about anyone. But whether or not it goes further is still up to the rest of you.

Autistic Spectrum

Red	Orange	Yellow	Green	Blue	Indigo	Violet
Inclination	Feelings	Personality Type	Sexuality	Abilities	Voluntary/Involuntary Behaviours	High Functioning Autism
Science	Anxiety	ADHD	Heterosexual	Academic	Tourette's	Cerebral Palsy
Music	Depression	ADD	A Sexual	Dyscalculia	Stammers	Downs Syndrome
Mathematics	PTSD	PDA	Bi Sexual	Dyspraxia	Addiction	Fragile X
Art/Creativity	Complex PTSD	PDD Non Specific	Gay	Dyslexia	Drugs	Global Developmental Delay
Languages	Complex Trauma	Aspergers Syndrome	Lesbian	Dysgraphia	Alcohol	Brain Tumours
Sport	Denial	Bipolar Disorder	Transgender	Face Recognition	Substances	Strokes
Business	Repression	Borderline Personality	Transsexual	Auditory	Gambling	Williams Syndrome
Social/Non Social	Projection	Schizophrenia	Paedophilia	Visual Processing	Shopping Addiction	Neurological Conditions
Communicator	Displacement	Paranoia	Polyamorous	Non Verbal	Sex Addiction	Rhett Syndrome
Reformer	Regression	Narcissism	Polyandrous	Emotional Intelligence	Eating Disorders	Multiple Sclerosis
Helper	Rationalisation	Histrionic	Queer	Speech/language	OCD	Motor Neurone Disease
Achiever	Sublimation	Avoidant	Homosexual	Visual Processing	Domestic Violence	Parkinson's Disease
Individualist	Reaction Formation	Dependent	Heterosexual	Delayed Processing	Pathological Behaviours	Alzheimer's
Investigator	Compartmentalisation	Schizoid	Pansexual	Sensory Sensitivities	Hayfever	Convulsions
Loyalist	Intellectualisation	Schizotypal	Polyandrous	Allergies	Migraine	Carpel Tunnel
Enthusiast		Anti Social	Intersex	Pain Threshold	Epilepsy	Lycanthropy
Peacemaker		Manipulator	Non binary		Asthma	
Challenger		Empath	Intersex		Suicidal Ideations	
Animals		Sociopathic	Gender non Specific		Extrovert/Introvert	
		Psychopathic	Gender Dysphoria		Moral Reasoning	
		Cluster Personalities				
		Dissociative Disorders				

Chapter 11

A Visual Over View

It's very hard to define what The Spectrum may actually look like. If you reflect on Chart 1 it may give you an over view of some of what the Spectrum may actually look like and the conditions or rather identities and traits of people's personas some of which may be hidden some of which may be visible in each person you meet or may already know.

The following explanation maybe easier to understand as a visual overview for us Aspies that prefer visual images. So if you imagine an umbrella and turn it upside down, the top of the umbrella where the base is, this is where all the spokes join together, and this is where you would use the term Autism.

Let's start with the fact that one or more of us may fall into having distinct personality traits related to with 'Genius' which appears as a pre disposition for a talent in one or more of the following 7 areas: Sport, Music, Languages, Business, Mathematics, Creativity, or Science. Sir Isaac Newton divided the colour Spectrum into 7 named colours: red, orange, yellow, green, blue, indigo, and violet. He chose 7 colours out of a belief derived from the ancient Greek sophists, of there being a connection between the colours, the musical notes, the known objects in the solar system, and the days of the week. Let's call this layer red. Just out of interest Isaac Newton was a mathematician, physicist, astronomer, theologian, and author so he had at least 4 red layers going on.

We may have a flair for business or languages which comes naturally to us, we may also be an excellent journalist with a flair for words that we have turned into a business writing that we earn money from as our career. Another example may be having a flair in mathematics so much so our 'genius' area becomes our chosen career as an accountant. Many of our genius traits contribute to become our chosen profession. This is where your natural ability falls, this is known as a person's executive functioning ability.

A person's natural ability is something that a person is more inclined to have a natural ability for in Sport, Science, Mathematics, Creativity, Languages, Business, and Music. You don't have to be a prodigy in these areas, it's just where your usual ability lies. Some people have an extra ability in one or more of these areas but you could be particularly sporty, be musically talented, have a flair for languages, be considered very artistically creative, have a mathematical brain prone to be good with numbers or be considered or scientifically knowledgeable compared to the average person, or they could have excellent business skills or acumen using creative flair or both so they can see potential ideas before anyone else can. You can have an inclination to be a social or non social person, or maybe you desire at times to be one or the other. If you feel that you enjoy silence and being reclusive away from the world or whether you like to be a party animal. Some Aspies may have an affinity or inclination to be sensitively creatively attuned to animals, other Aspies may not. Along with being a social or non social individual, will be the aspect of being a communicator, these skills determine your levels of engagement with others and your opportunity as an Aspie to engage with society as you see fit. Other inclinations of personality include whether you see yourself as a reformer or perfectionist, helper or giver, achiever or performer, individualist or romanticist investigator or observer, loyalist or skeptic, enthusiast or epicure, challenger or protector, peacemaker or mediator.

Anxiety and Depression now if you take this as the second layer on the Spectrum, lets choose the Spectrum colour for this layer as orange, knowing that at some point in your life you are going to experience these feelings due to the fact that anxiety will be the surface layers, and depression is going to take the deeper feelings of un earthed sediment emotional feelings that you have not have dealt with which need to come to the surface.

Anxiety and Depression are symptoms of an Autistic Spectrum's way of thinking, a person's reaction to the environment they find themselves in, where they are overwhelmed and unable to cope bringing on these symptoms or bi product behaviours of the term Autism. From Anxiety and Depression can spring suicidal thoughts which become a one track tunnel vision feeling there is no other way out of the thought process that the person is feeling and experiencing.

We would liken it to going down the rabbit hole and not being able to find your way back with ease, where the brain can't process other solutions to a problem, alternatively certain instances thoughts feelings and behaviours are a cry for attention to say "Hey look at me I can't cope I am over whelmed", a reaction to life events and in life cycle circumstances. Anxiety and Depression will be systematic and unavoidable and all three can happen in cycles and, they are the body's warning mechanism that they are experiencing things they can no longer control as an adverse side effect. Sometimes suicidal thoughts feelings and behaviours may happen once in a person's life time or can fluctuate throughout the day depending on the individual's brain processing. This can also be due to a chemical imbalance.

Also in this orange section of feelings we could put (PTSD) Post Traumatic Stress Disorder. PTSD is now classified as a mental disorder that can develop after a person is exposed to a traumatic event such as, sexual assault, warfare, traffic collision, child abuse, domestic abuse, attack, accident, or trauma related incident. Symptoms include disturbing thoughts, feelings, dreams, flashbacks, or real time events which can relate the individual back to events and to the mental, physical distress of the original event that caused the trauma. These symptoms can last for a month or years after the event.

Complex PTSD is a psychological disorder that can develop in response to prolonged repeated experiences of interpersonal trauma in a context where the individual has little or no chance of escape. Some examples include sexual, psychological and physical abuse, neglect,, chronic intimate partner violence, kidnapping, and hostage situations, slavery, human trafficking, prisoners of war, defectors of cults or situations involving captivity or entrapment lacking in viable escape routes. C - PTSD symptoms include prolonged feelings of terror, worthlessness, helplessness and deformation of one's identity and sense of self. Different scientific researchers believe that C - PTSD is similar to dissociative identity disorder and borderline personality disorder because of the distortions in a person's core identity and emotional dysregulation and somatization (a tendency to experience and communicate psychological distress in the form of bodily symptoms and seek medical help for them).

Denial, is a defence mechanism whereby people avoid acknowledging that there is a problem. What is important is not that people recognise their denial but they are able to accept what they are feeling that leads to the denial in the first place. Denial is a cognitive process that is an attempt to alter our experiences of unwanted or unacceptable emotions. It is tempting to say that denial could appear to be a form of mental illness but someone with an acute mental illness may not be thinking clearly enough to consciously choose denial, they maybe experiencing lack of insight or awareness.

Repression of painful memories and unsavoury thoughts, or irrational beliefs can upset you. Instead of facing them you may unconsciously choose to hide them in the hope of forgetting about them entirely. This does not mean that you these memories will disappear entirely, as they influence behaviours and impact future relationships and you may not realise the impact that this defence mechanism is having.

Projection is when you may have a thought or feeling about another person and you may feel uncomfortable. If you project those feelings you are misattributing them to another person. You see in their actions the things you wish you could do or say.

Displacement is when you direct strong emotions and frustrations towards a person or object that is not threatening, this allows you the satisfaction of an impulse to react without risking significant consequences. For example if you get angry with your child or spouse because you had a bad day at work, it is easier and less problematic than reacting to your boss.

Regression is when if people feel threatened or anxious then unconsciously escape to an earlier stage of development. For example, in young children if they experience trauma and loss they may suddenly act younger again by wetting the bed or thumb sucking. Adults can regress to by over eating certain foods, chain smoking, chewing on pencils or pens, or avoiding every day activities.

Rationalisation - this inclination allows you to feel comfortable with a choice you make even if you know on another level if it's not right for you.

Sublimation is a very positive strategy. Instead of lashing out at your employees, for example, you choose to channel your frustrations into kick boxing, exercise, music, art, or sport for example.

Reaction Formation is a feeling that people choose to behave in the opposite manner to their instincts, for example instead of feeling angry or frustrated people choose to react in an overly positive way.

Compartmentalisation is when we separate our lives into independent sections in a way to cope and protect many elements of it. For example if you choose not to discuss personal issues at work.

Intellectualisation is when you are given a situation and you may choose to remove all emotion from your responses and just focus on the facts.

The third layer of The Spectrum may look like we may have personality traits functioning in the Asperger's Syndrome (AS), Attention Deficit Hyper Activity (ADHD), Attention Deficit (ADD), Narcissism (NP), Obsessive Compulsive (OCD), Bi Polar (BPD), Borderline (BP), Pathological Demand Avoidance (PDA) Sociopathic (SP) and

Psychopathic (PP) which appear in our behaviours.

Let's choose the Spectrum colour of yellow, only you actually know what your behaviours actually look like and those closest to you. The traits are described in earlier chapters, these are ones you may recognise, these maybe symptoms you have not yet had a diagnosis for or they may be a traits not yet mentioned yet in this book.

They all could fall into this category? Asperger's syndrome which has been discussed in previous chapters has been defined as a collective group of behaviours and characteristics which is varying in nature due the intensity of the characteristics. PDD NOS (pervasive developmental disorder non specified) is where the characteristics and behaviours are non specified ie: they do not fall into any of the groups as defined.

PDA (Pathelogical Demand Avoidance) as described in Chapter 3 is defined by a distinct range of autistic behaviours where resistance and an avoidance to do certain every day tasks is characterised by anxiety). (ADHD) Attention Deficit Hyper Activity Disorder is characterised by inattention, hyperactivity, and impulsivity. Bipolar, Borderline, Schizophrenic, Paranoid, Phobic, Narcissistic, Histrionic, Avoidant, Dependent, Manipulation, Schizoid, Schizotypal, Anti Social, OCD, Empath, Sociopathic, Psychopathic.

Bi Polar disorder, previously known as manic depression, is a mental health disorder that causes periods of depression and periods of elevated mood known as mania or hyper mania, or sometimes symptoms of psychosis may be present. The risk of suicide is greater with people with Bi Polar and the risk of self harm can occur in 30-40%. Borderline personality is also known as emotionally unstable personality, with an unstable sense of self, unstable emotions and self harm. People with this condition struggle with a sense of emptiness and fears of abandonment and people may also have eating disorders with this condition. Schizophrenia, is a severe long term mental health condition causing different psychological symptoms it is a type of psychosis where a person may not be able to distinguish there own thoughts and ideas from reality. Symptoms include hallucinations, delusions, muddled thoughts and changes in behaviour.

Paranoid personality is a pervasive and long standing suspiciousness and general mistrust of others, they think they are in danger and look for signs and threats of that danger not appreciating any other evidence. A Phobia is an extreme or irrational fear or dislike of a specified thing or group of things. Narcissistic personality is a long term pattern of behaviour characterised by exaggerated feelings of self importance excessive need for admiration and a lack of empathy. Those affected often spend time thinking about achieving power or success or in their appearance; they often take advantage of the people around them. Whereby, a Histrionic personality is characterised by a pattern of excessive attention seeking emotions including seductive behaviour and excessive need for approval. Manipulation aims to change the behaviour or perception of others through indirect deceptiveness or underhanded tactics, usually by advancing the interests of the manipulator, usually often at another's expense. Such methods could be considered exploitative devious and controlling for power and gain.

Avoidant or Anxious Personality those affected display a patter of severe social anxiety, social inhibition, feelings of inadequacy, inferiority and extreme sensitivity to negative evaluation and rejection. They avoid social interaction despite a strong desire for intimacy. Whereby a Dependent personality is a pervasive psychological dependence on other people to meet there emotional and physical needs with only a small minority achieving normal levels of independence. Characterised by excessive fear and anxiety from extreme passivity, devastation or helplessness when relationships end manifesting in avoidance of relationships, responsibilities and severe submission.

Schizoid personality is characterised by a lack of interest in social relationships with a tendency towards a solitary or sheltered lifestyle of secrecy, emotional coldness, detachment and apathy where individuals may be unable to form intimate relationships and create a rich elaborate internal fantasy world. Schizotypal is characterised by severe social anxiety, thought disorder, paranoid ideation, and transient psychosis with regular unconventional beliefs they may react oddly in conversations, peculiar modes of speech and dress are symptoms.

An anti social personality is often characterised by a long term pattern of disregard for the rights, or violation of the rights of others with a low moral sense of conscience, usually categorised by a history of crime, legal problems or impulsive aggressive behaviour. Anti social personality behaviour also includes psychopathic and sociopathic characteristics with impaired empathy and remorse and ego tistical traits.

All the above personality traits, have a full or partial tunnel vision of not being able to see the bigger picture or viewpoint perspective of the effects of their behaviour. Usually the behaviours appear unbalanced not equal where the behaviour impacts other people and the world around them and the individual exhibiting them is unable to see how the behaviour could change or its impact on the people around them especially where an individual's perspective can be considered narrow.

Cognitive Behavioural Therapy (CBT) a form of counselling or psychotherapy is thought to help these types of thought processes, the results can be short lived or permanent depending on how severe the thought process is manifested in the persons brain pattern. CBT can challenge the thought process and evidence irrational thoughts, ideas and behaviours but if the conditional has a genetic predisposition and the behaviours are too ingrained the results may only be temporary.

This list is not exhaustive and you may find that there are more that fall into this range. If you identify as one of these types of personality and behaviours. As these personality types are not consistent 24/7 and you may show certain traits throughout the day or lunar cycle usually as a reaction to your environment or everyday situations that you may find yourself in.

These traits can be especially noticeable around friends or family or you may or may not notice them at all as they part of your personality and may be considered completely normal part of your personality, its only when they start to become a problem to you and your everyday life is it time to possibly get a diagnosis if you feel it will help you.

Many of us have been coping in this yellow spectrum section for years and our coping mechanisms may have become completely unhealthy, as in other colour areas of the spectrum we have to learn healthier options that are structured more for us. This could include being more organised, thinking more of others and being less selfish, we call it widening the lens a little and in many cases perhaps seeking out professional help to do that by way of a psychologist or therapist.

Now onto the fourth layer of the Spectrum is your Gender or sexuality, let's use the Spectrum colour Green. Whether you are straight heterosexual, gay, lesbian, bi sexual, A sexual, transgender or gender dysphoria. As mentioned in the chapter on sexuality only you know what your gender type is and where you fit on the Spectrum. Sexuality can be defined as many colours of the rainbow but in this instance we are using the shade of green, at present there is A Sexual, Bi Sexual, Gay, Lesbian, Transgender, Transsexual, Paedophilia, Polyamorous, Queer, Homosexual, Heterosexual, Pansexual, Polyandrous, Intersex, Non binary, androgynous. This list is not comprehensive and can make for further allowances of other genders that do not necessarily fall into a specific type as discussed in the chapter on sexuality.

A person's sexuality has never been thought of as part of an Autistic brain before but findings on the frequency of Individuals with ASD seem to have more hypersexual and paraphilic fantasies (known as a sexual perversion or deviation) and behaviours than general population studies suggest. Studies suggest that many individuals with ASD seek sexual and romantic relationships similar to the non ASD population and have the entire Spectrum of sexual experiences and behaviours. However, there are still many stereotypes and societal beliefs about individuals with ASD, referring to them as uninterested in social and romantic relationships and as being A sexual. There is evidence that some ASD individuals are possibly more tolerant toward same sex relationships, depending on how flexible their thinking actually is. If they are rigid thinkers on the spectrum then same sex relationships will be intolerable a factor in some homophobic hate crime. It could be possible that ASD individuals choose their sexual preferences more independently of what is socially accepted or demanded, maybe partly due to a lower sensitivity to social norms or gender roles. So far, there are almost no existent studies about paraphilias in the ASD population. However, almost all case studies addressed paraphilic behaviours in male ASD individuals with some kind of cognitive impairment.

The fifth layer of the Spectrum – Perceptions includes sensitivities and your abilities in levels of coping mechanisms to the environment these can include skin sensitivities to products, metals fabric clothing etc, diet, celiac, dairy intolerant, food intolerance, sensitivity Issues to food, light, heat, noise, cold, over stimulation to light, noise, sight, the atmosphere and the environment by way of allergies. You could be more likely to experience a hearing impediment either from birth or reduced hearing in later life. You could develop hay fever or asthma in later life due to the environment and your sensitivity within it.

In this fifth layer, coloured blue range, dyspraxia, discalculia, dyslexia and hyperlexia, face recognition, photographic memory, auditory processing, visual processing, clairvoyance, spiritual abilities, non verbal abilities, emotional intelligence, speech and language. (clairvoyancy and spiritual attunement is a natural ability to the environment that you can tune in to a receive vibrations from another sphere). This fifth segment of the Spectrum umbrella looks at your sensitivities and abilities they may actually not be a difficulty and in some people it may be an advantage to have this ability, this can be likened to the senses so if one sense is not working in one area the senses of the other areas over compensate. For example, there may be someone with dyslexia, they may not be able to read write or comprehend words too well but they may have above average intellect and a very high IQ because they process information differently. We may struggle in everyday life and have found different coping mechanisms that may put us at a distinct advantage over normal so called learners. Other learning impairments include, dyscalculia, dyspraxia, dyslexia, dysgraphia, face recognition, auditory processing, visual processing, colour blindness, non verbal, deaf mutism or hard of hearing, or high or low emotional intelligence, sensory processing, executive functioning Or they may have trouble recognizing other people's feelings and "reading" nonverbal cues. This is when people tend to be very literal and don't always understand puns, riddles or figures of speech. These symptoms are also seen with social communication disorder, and receptive language issues. In difficulties with executive function, Some people find it hard to get organised and solve problems. They can struggle to keep their emotions in check and change the way they do things without getting upset. A tendency to be clumsy and uncoordinated they may have trouble with handwriting, riding a bike, catching a ball or running or they may experience trouble working with words. Many people may struggle to express themselves, follow conversations, and speak with the right volume and inflection. These are also symptoms of speech language issues and nonverbal learning disabilities.

There's a lot of overlap in the symptoms of autism and learning and attention issues. Autism and learning abilities can occur together. But autism itself is not necessarily an disability. The main struggle involves social understanding, communication and repetitive routines or behaviours including narrow and obsessive interests. For instance, a person with visual processing issues may stand too close to someone during conversation because he has trouble judging distances and he has a poor sense of personal space doesn't necessarily mean he cannot process information, he has learnt to compensate with his abilities to get the best out of himself. Delayed processing also falls into this category, sometimes sensory issues, and sensitivities, etc can slow an individual s processing down and whilst they may appear slower to comprehend than other people it's because their senses are reacting to other information first. Lastly pain tolerance, some people have extreme pain tolerance, others don't feel hot or cold temperatures and walk around with T shirts in Winter, others can fall and not feel pain.

The sixth layer of the Spectrum could be classed as voluntary and involuntary behaviours. Let's colour this layer of the Spectrum Indigo. Behaviours in the indigo layer include Tourette's, stammers, addiction, gambling, drugs, alcohol, sexual behaviour, shopping, eating, domestic abuse, OCD anger, victim, hoarding, phobias, allergies and pathological behaviours.

This segment of the chart following on from a person's ability type will be voluntary and involuntary behaviours for example, having an addictive or non addictive personality in one or more of the following areas of addiction, drugs, alcohol, various other substances, gambling, shopping, sexual behaviours, eating disorders, bulmenia, anorexia, pica, avoidant or restrictive food intake, pulling or picking disorder, and domestic violence and abuse, pathological behaviours for eg: lying and or your moral reasoning skills, whereby OCD is a mental disorder in which a person feels the need to perform certain routines repeatedly called compulsions or has certain thoughts repeatedly called obsessions the individual is unable to control either the thoughts or the behaviours associated with them. Other conditions associated with this section include tics, Migraines, Epilepsy, Asthma, Hayfever (Allergies) and Suicidal Ideations, all fall into this sector of voluntary or involuntary behaviours of which we may or may not have control. Whether we are extroverted in personality or whether we are introverted, or possess morals and codes of conduct.

You could argue about whether these behaviours are indeed genetic or a learned behaviour, whether they are voluntary or involuntary, the fact is that they are all centred around power reward and control and are to do more with the functioning of an Autistic brain as many of the behaviours are very similar but they are obsessive behaviours subject to the object of control and power, where the subject matter is generic. These personality behaviours have never been included before into the Autistic Spectrum as very little research has been conducted in these specific areas and the way science is moving to combine all the future research in these areas we are a long way off from achieving both mathematical evidence and data. We hope that that if significant research was done in these areas it would provide us with the necessary evidence that we see in peoples behaviours.

The seventh and final layer on the Spectrum is Affiliations to Autism - conditions at present with a medical diagnosis. Let's call this colour violet on the Spectrum of colours. These have not been touched on in depth this book largely for the fact because they are all complex conditions that need whole chapters in writing, but could include Cerebral Palsy, Epilepsy, Fragile X, Global Developmental Delay, Williams Syndrome, Rhett Syndrome, Multiple Sclerosis, Motor Neurone Disease, Parkinsons Disease, Neurological Conditions, Brain Tumours Carpel Tunnel and Lycanthropy, and many other conditions, too many to list and many yet science has yet to prove. ASD refers to a group of complex neurodevelopment disorders characterised by repetitive and characteristic patterns of behaviour and difficulties and affect daily functioning. Some children and adults with ASD are fully able to perform all activities of daily living while others require substantial support to perform basic activities. Some of the behavioural traits mentioned so far in this book do fall into this category but the difference is here the violet section of the spectrum are severe needing supported medical assistance and intervention. You could argue that a drug addict or severe alcoholic need daily constant intervention and I would suggest that that is when the blue behaviours are going into the violet spectrum colour behaviours.

Some examples of Affiliated conditions include Cerebral Palsy, Fragile X, Williams Syndrome, Rhett Syndrome, Multiple Sclerosis, Parkinsons Disease, Motor Neuron Disease, Vertigo, Brain Tumours, Strokes, Convulsions, Alzheimer's and Carpel Tunnel Syndrome are a few of the more minor conditions, but all Neurological conditions, there are far too many for me to list all individual types but you will understand that these are linked to Autism brain conditions.

NINDS (National Institute of Neurological Diseases) researchers are studying aspects of brain function and development that are altered in people with ASD. For example, NINDS funded researchers are investigating the formation and function of neuronal synapses, the sites of communication between neurons, which may not properly operate in ASD and neurodevelopmental disorders. Other studies use brain imaging a highly contested area often providing illusions of data in people with and without ASD to identify differences in brain connectivity and activity patterns associated with features of ASD. Researchers hope that understanding these alterations can help identify new opportunities for therapeutic interventions, but sadly research is slow.

Global Developmental Delay (GDD) is the general term used to describe a condition that occurs during the developmental period of a child between birth and 18 years. It is usually defined by the child being diagnosed with having a lower intellectual functioning than what is perceived as 'normal'. Global development delay and learning disability. For some people, the delay in their development will be short term and can be overcome with additional support or therapy. In other cases the delay may be more significant and they will need ongoing support. Other terms associated with this condition are failure to thrive (which focuses on lack of weight gain and physical development), intellectual disability (which focuses on intellectual deficits and the changes they cause to development) and developmental disability (which can refer to both intellectual and physical disability altering development).

Lastly we can't not mention the rare condition of lycanthropy. Lycanthropy can be caused by a physical imbalance in the brain. Particular areas of the brain, specifically in the cerebral cortex, responsible for a person's perception of their own body. Some examples of Lycanthropy include Parrot Man. Bird lover and self-described "Parrotman" Ted Richards had his face tattooed with feathers, cut off his ears and risked going blind by having his eyes coloured with ink... First, the self-described "Parrotman" had his face tattooed to look like he has feathers in the five colours of his parrots his home in Bristol UK is described a s being a human cage to many parrots as he considers himself one of them.

Erik Sprague known professionally as The Lizardman, is an American freak show and sideshow performer. He is best known for his body modification, including his sharpened teeth, full-body tattoo of green scales, bifurcated tongue, subdermal implants and green-inked lips. Erik recently gained the official Guinness World Record for 'Most weight lifted and swung from the ear lobes' on the set of 'Lo Show dei Record' in Milan, Italy on 19 Jun 2014. Other examples include Cat Woman, and Vampire Woman whereby Some modern researchers have tried to explain the reports of Werewolf behaviour with recognised medical conditions such as schizophrenia. Lycathropy has dated as far back as biblical times. It has been associated with the altered states of mind that accompany psychosis (the mental state that typically involves delusions and hallucinations) with the transformation only seeming to happen in the mind and behaviour of the affected person.

Now that all the sections of the Spectrum umbrella are complete the sections overlap and interchange with each other for example you may be a bi sexual narcissistic gambling addict with dyspraxia who suffers mild depression and high anxiety when he doesn't win at online addiction gaming. This is but one example, but if you look at patterns more closely especially how patterns run through families and we will use the very well known Donald Trump as a case study for reflection, as he is in the public eye. You might argue that Donald Trump is heterosexual, narcissist, sex addict, a compulsive liar, a fabulous manipulator, with verbal reasoning skills even though his views maybe rather dichotomous. His older brother Fred Jr became a severe chronic alcoholic and died at an early age. What we know about addicts is that they are highly intelligent but their moral reasoning skills go out the window where addiction is concerned he probably had undiagnosed ADHD. His older sister Maryanne Trump Barry is a former judge and lawyer so she has a strong moral ethical code and highly academic organised and disciplined with a high intellect. His other sister Elizabeth Trump Grau is more isolated and reclusive than her brothers, enjoyment of the limelight and she was a banker so she had strong mathematical tendencies. Little is known about his younger brother Robert Trump and his personality traits but like his older sister Elizabeth he is more isolated and shuns the limelight.

What this example is key to show you is that all siblings and family members will display key notes of autism along the spectrum kind of like a pick n mix of personalities via genetic it's the luck of the draw and the environment of what you may be predisposed to or what you may have a weakness or strength in. But most importantly now we have managed to categorise it by colour what colours of the spectrum are you and where do you fit in?

Chapter 12

Conclusion with Questions and Answers

Our brain is the most powerful muscle we have to over think things and let's face it if our brains functioning is slightly different than other people on the spectrum it will become a natural tendency. To compensate this let's look at our actualising tendency, but what does this actually mean? It means that we have an inherent capacity to self heal or self right our selves. We all have it within us to have the capacity to sort themselves out - we find answers to our own problems, in the same way that our body heals physical injuries deep inside us is a capacity to wards psychological healing, maintenance and growth. As we know at some level this is right for us, we possess an organismic wisdom that can help us deal with the most challenging of circumstances. We don't need to depend on others to look at our bettering ourselves, we are the authorities of our own lives with helpful insight.

But if we've got such a deep tendency towards healing and growth, how is it we can get so lost and f%£cked up in our lives? Why do people end up addicted to drugs, depressed, self harm, self sabotaging battering themselves psychologically or physically or by chasing money that drives them into an early grave? There's a pretty coherent answer to this, because we instead of trusting our own inner wisdom, we end up being moulded by the outside world. So for example we believe that the most important thing is a Rolex watch or thousands of Facebook friends, a bigger and better car, a holidays, houses, designer clothes and we come to ignore our internal voice because we are wanting to have fun, and we as Aspies are wanting to fit in, be creative. We develop what's known as 'external' locus of evaluation as opposed to an internal one.

There is evidence to support that we feel happier and more satisfied when our intrinsic goals are met rather than our extrinsic ones. But our actualising tendencies get scuppered by outside world values, and we as individuals become 'victims' of our external circumstances.

But when we get lost, is it really true that we always know what's right for us? We have a deep intuitive feeling about where we need to be and its almost always spot on. But sometimes our intuitive feeling takes us in the wrong direction, and this is what we need to learn from. As growth and learning come from an assimilation of fitting the external world to what we already know and accommodating or adapting our way of seeing the world to what we learn from the outside. We would call this more a shades of grey theory as opposed to black or white thinking. As us Aspies tend to think wither on one end of the spectrum being black or the other end being white and forget totally about all the other shades of grey in between. We would focus on our inner wisdom as opposed to the wisdom of others or the outside world and it would all seem rather one sided.

In life we are always on the way to somewhere, through knowledge, life lessons, life experience, which is why you bought this book because you wanted answers to a huge question. We try to act intelligently in the best way we know how, looking for different possibilities rather than being completely sponge like, mechanical or robotic we can only know what we most fundamentally want and need in our lives. Which is why it is important, to step back from guidance and advice so we can naturally allow our own self righting force to come to the forefront. Therefore understanding ourselves as self healing human beings is a great reminder of the incredible creativity and wisdom that we Aspies have in finding our own answers.

I don't feel that I fit in anywhere on what this book describes what do I do next?

As we state at the start of the book "A Spectrum is used to classify something in terms of its position on a scale between two extreme points". Your feelings thoughts behaviours may fall somewhere in between, if you have identified some behaviours in your life that you tend to become anxious about, then it's best to write them down and see if there are other behaviours that may fall into spectrum type behaviours. You may have a perfectionism trait, you may have un realistic expectations of others or yourself, you may need regular down time because of life over load. What ever your behaviours are its best to seek professional help and start by discussing them with your GP first and foremost. The traits identified in this book are not yet 'officially' linked to the Autistic Spectrum as of yet and what we are suggesting is that these traits display behaviours that *could be* spectrum linked.

I thought everyone on the Autistic Spectrum had a disability? I am not disabled so therefore I am not on the Spectrum right?

For the terms of this books content we have not included Spectrum linked medical disabilities that are already widely known about for example Cerebal Palsy, Fragile X, Downs Syndrome, Epilepsy, Rhett Syndrome, Visual and Hearing Impairments and Fetal anti-convulsant syndrome. We are not here to minimise any autistic diagnosis that has a severe learning disability element. Far from it, we are trying to raise awareness of the other aspects of the spectrum that may have been not scientifically researched as yet. Cognitive impairments such as those highlighted in the book can be quite disabling for the people who experience them. Whilst they may not be appear visibly noticeable to other people, but for the people experiencing them they can be very disabling.

At this rate we will all be classed as Autistic and have a label?

There is an increased rate of Autism diagnosis in adults as opposed to children, in the last few years yes, as increasing numbers of our children are being diagnosed there are whole generations of adults, parents, grandparents and great grandparents uncles and aunts who have similar behavioural traits who've never been diagnosed at all. The phenomenon of Autistic patients who complain about not fitting in, social awkwardness, perfectionism or obsessive traits may find comfort understanding why they feel the way they feel. We believe this Autism 'epidemic' it is largely down to the reclassification of ASD, and more and more criteria for diagnosis is broadening the criteria as we are become more scientifically aware of the condition and what it includes. There are more variations of symptoms and behaviours and as a straight-line assumption the bar for diagnosis has become progressively lower over the last 50 years following a more lower diagnostic curve. Within the next decade there will be no one with a clear distinction between someone with the condition and the average person and we will all be classed as Autistic, especially now including some of the extra information in this book, to include personality disorders, eating disorders, different sexuality, learning disabilities, addictions, phobias, compulsions and domestic violence.

This is a desperate situation for those people who have profound, extreme high functioning Autism who are disabled by their condition and for their families. It causes widespread misunderstanding of how serious it can be.

For many adults and children who are a little bit different or showing behavioural issues, it is easier to accept that this is linked to a disorder of some kind rather than accepting this is who they are. It also helps absolve guilt that you may feel if you or a child is struggling to fit in with his or your peers. In effect the label of Autism is a neat convenient way of explaining complex reasons of brain impairment when an individual doesn't confirm to societal expectations. To simplify this further you wouldn't go to the supermarket and buy random nameless tins without labels on bring them home and store them in your cupboard, take pot luck when you're hungry, open a tin expecting baked beans when in fact it's a sponge pudding. The same goes for labelling when we have a list of ingredients on our labels, we know what we are getting and if some one has an allergy or doesn't like a particular ingredient then they know to either avoid it or not eat it, or choose something different depending on their mood. The same applies to Autism we all have behavioural traits that are good and bad and indifferent, once we are aware of what they are we are then are more able to have self awareness and choice.

Why is this book not evidence based about such a scientific subject as Autism?

This is a really a good question and one that I thought long and hard about before beginning this project. We decided that an evidence based scientific book for professionals was already out there in many different forms covering many different topics by leading experts and pioneers in the field on some not all of the traits that are included in this one, but collectively there seemed no link to all of the behavioural traits and no way of Science to prove all of this traits exist across one single condition except individually. Because of this factor we decided to make this type of information more accessible to you, the individual, so you would understand it and it would be less scientific as Autism is highly complex with many different factors involved. Whilst we have not included all of the personality traits and behaviours we have included some of the main ones that have not been linked to Autism yet and we believe that we wanted you the reader to decide for yourself if their appeared strong enough evidential links in the patterns of behaviour. If this book had been written with clinical evidence it would have attracted a different readership entirely and lots of questions would still be being asked out there by people who have many of the patterns of behaviour but no answers as to why. We decided to write this book as a self help publication, simplifying many of the complicated labels what Autism actually is.

What we've also done in this book is describe what the Autistic Spectrum may actually look like, what it may be composed of as no leading scientific evidence based formula or theory can actually state what the Spectrum may actually look like and us Aspies need to be creative in our visual understanding things. We hope that it helps you.

Is this Autism or is it different personality types or a personality disorders - I am confused?

Doctors use guidelines for diagnosing mental health problems. The main guidelines are the International Classification of Diseases (ICD-10) produced by the World Health Organisation (WHO), and Diagnostic and Statistical Manual (DSM-5) produced by the American Psychiatric Association. The guidelines usually say which symptoms you may have and for how long you should have them to get a particular diagnosis. A doctor (such as a psychiatrist) will ask you questions about your life and what sort of feelings, emotions, and behaviours you have. This is called an 'assessment'.

You should never feel as though it is your fault, or that you are to blame if you have been diagnosed with a personality disorder. Personality disorders diagnoses are grouped into three 'clusters', A, B, and C.

People with Cluster A personality disorders can find it hard to relate to other people. Their behaviour might seem odd or eccentric to other people. A Paranoid personality disorder – Is if you may feel very suspicious of others but without a reason if you have been diagnosed with paranoid personality disorder. This can make you feel other people are lying to you or using you. This can make it difficult to trust others, even friends. You may find it difficult to forgive insults and will bear grudges. If you feel this may be you your doctor should rule out schizophrenia, psychosis, and mood disorders if you have been diagnosed with paranoid personality disorder.

Schizoid personality disorder you may have few social relationships and will prefer to be alone. You might actually be very shy, but other people may think you are quite cold and distant. Schizotypal personality disorder is where you have difficulty forming relationships with other people. You may have strange thoughts, feel paranoid and see or hear things that aren't there. You may also lack emotion or be described as being 'eccentric'.

Cluster B personality disorders can find it hard to control their emotions. Other people might see them as unpredictable. Examples include; Antisocial personality disorder (ASPD). Being diagnosed with antisocial personality disorder (ASPD) may mean you are impulsive, reckless and do not think about how your actions affect other people. You may get easily frustrated, aggressive and be prone to violence. You may do things to get what you want. Others may see this as acting selfishly and without guilt.

Borderline personality disorder (BPD).You may have strong emotions, mood swings, and feelings you find difficult to cope with if you have borderline personality disorder (BPD). You may feel anxious and distressed a lot of the time. You may have problems with how you see yourself and your identity. You may self-harm or use drugs and alcohol to cope with these feelings. This can affect the relationships you have with other people. BPD is also known as 'emotionally unstable personality disorder'.

A Histrionic personality disorder, If you are diagnosed with histrionic personality disorder, you may like being the centre of attention. You may feel anxious about being ignored. This can cause you to be lively and over-dramatic. You may become bored with normal routines, worry a lot about your appearance and want to be noticed. This is different from a Narcissistic personality disorder. Narcissistic personality disorder can mean you have a high sense of self importance. You may fantasise about unlimited success and want attention and admiration. You may feel you are more entitled to things than other people are. You might act selfishly to gain success. You may do this because inside, you don't feel significant or important.

Cluster C personality disorders. People with Cluster C personality disorders have strong feelings of fear or anxiety. They might appear withdrawn to other people. These include; Dependent personality disorder. If you have dependent personality disorder, you may allow other people to take responsibility for parts of your life. You may not have much self confidence, or be unable to do things alone. You may find that you put your own needs after the needs of others. You may feel hopeless or fear being alone.

An Avoidant personality disorder, If you have avoidant personality disorder, you may have a fear of being judged negatively. This can cause you to feel uncomfortable in social situations. You might not like criticism, worry a lot and have low self-esteem. You may want affection, but worry that you will be rejected.

Obsessive compulsive personality disorder, If you have this condition, you may feel anxious about things that seem unorganised or 'messy'. Everything you do must be just right, and nothing can be left to chance. You may be very cautious about things and think a lot about small details. Others may see you as being controlling. Obsessive compulsive personality disorder is different to obsessive compulsive disorder (OCD). If you have obsessive compulsive personality disorder, you may believe your actions are justified. People with OCD tend to realise that their behaviour is not rational.

There is no single approach to treating personality disorders. If your GP feels you have a complex personality disorder, they may refer you to a community mental health team, or specialist personality disorder service or unit, if there is one locally. These services are made up of professionals such as psychologists, psychiatrists and therapists who will have experience in helping people with personality disorders. Sometimes you can contact these services yourself to get support. You and your doctor or healthcare team should agree on a treatment plan that works best for you. One-to-one and group psychological treatments or 'talking therapies' are often recommended. They all involve talking with a therapist, but are different from one another. The options for treating personality disorders are continuously developing.

Everyone has different ways of thinking, feeling, and behaving. It is these thoughts, feelings, and behaviours that make up our 'personality'. These are often called our traits. They shape the way we view the world and the way we relate to others. By the time we are adults these will make us part of who we are.

You can think of your traits as sitting along a scale which is what we tried to do in writing this book. For example, everyone may feel emotional, get jealous, or want to be liked at times. But it is when these traits start to cause problems that you may be diagnosed as having a personality disorder.

A personality disorder can affect how you cope with life, manage relationships, and feel emotionally. You may find that your beliefs and ways of dealing with day-to-day life are different from others and that you find it difficult to change them. You may find your emotions confusing, tiring, and hard to control. This can be distressing for you and others. Because it is distressing, you may find that you develop other mental health problems like depression or anxiety. You may also do other things such as drink heavily, use drugs, or self-harm to cope. Research shows that personality disorders are fairly common. Many people live with some form of personality disorder.

I feel I fit some of the mild criteria does that mean I have mild autism and should I pay for a private diagnosis?

For some people I would suggest it's a way of medicalising certain behaviours or feelings that prevent them from functioning comfortably, socially, within the family setting, or in the work place, and if it helps them understand and accept the condition then I'd say why not, but it won't change who they are. If you recognise yourself in parts of this book and feel that by a professional diagnosis is the way forward for you personally and you need that formal clarification then that is up to you. This book is designed not to over generalise and open the flood gates for a stampede of self referrals to the health service, it was designed for you to as an individual to have a self awareness of who you are and what may be the causes. We can't change 100% of our character traits but what we can do is recognise them and hopefully self awareness will be the key to unlock doors in our lives to promote greater understanding of who and what we are as unique individuals. At the present moment the UK National Health Service does do adult diagnosis but the period of waiting for assessment is time consuming and because of the criteria needed for diagnosis it can be quiet a lengthy process. If a diagnosis has been made and medication for eg: Bipolar or ADHD is given it can take some time to get the medication levels correct for each individual so you may be waiting a little time. However if you feel that it is something you want to do then go for it, only you know you.

I don't recognise myself in any of this book I thought only boys had it does that mean I am not on the Spectrum?

Autism has many different forms, some with instantly recognisable traits others with less so. The first school of thought by health professionals was that unless the behavioural traits affected your day to day life and impacted you severly then you were not on the Spectrum. Many leading health professionals then went on to describe individuals as NT individuals - NT is short for neurotypical and is often used to refer to people who are not on the Autism Spectrum. It is a combination of the words "neurological" and "typical". But as more and more behavioural traits are being linked to the condition we would suggest that you are on there somewhere its just where abouts on it you actually fit. We tried to colour code it into classifications so it would be easier to understand and a base to start, some traits may be so mild they are hardly recognisable but others can impact day to day life. Some people are not diagnosed until later in life - and then only because they wanted confirmation of what they had figured out for themselves over the previous decade. Most of their lives, they have evaded a diagnosis by forcing themselves to stop doing things that parents and others found strange or unacceptable.

Some people develope tricks and coping mechanisms without realising it to mask Autism - for example, staring at the spot between someone's eyes instead of into their eyes, which makes them feel uncomfortable. Being anxious, nervousness, too, is hidden, the intense social and communication difficulties they experience almost daily, some can express themselves far easily in writing, but becomes disoriented during face-to-face communication where the immediacy of the interaction messes with processing ability so having time to think is always helpful..

To compensate, people may practice how to act. Before attending a social situation, for example, to keep a dialogue going, they might drop in a few well-rehearsed catchphrases, such as "good grief" or "go big or go home." If you do the nods, people won't lose interest. Over the past few years, scientists have discovered that, many people women included on the Spectrum 'camouflage' the signs of their Autism. This masking may explain at least in part why three to four times as many boys as girls are diagnosed with the condition. It might also account for why girls diagnosed young tend to show severe traits, and highly intelligent girls are often diagnosed late. (Men on the spectrum also camouflage, researchers have found, but not as commonly as women.)

Nearly everyone makes small adjustments to fit in better or conform to social norms, but camouflaging calls for constant and elaborate effort. It can help both men and women with Autism maintain their relationships and careers, but those gains often come at a heavy cost, including physical exhaustion and extreme anxiety. Camouflaging is often about a desperate and sometimes subconscious survival battle, camouflaging often develops as a natural adaptation strategy to navigate reality, so for many people, it's not until they get properly diagnosed, recognised and accepted that they can fully map out who they are.

Even so, not all people who camouflage say they would have wanted to know about their Autism earlier and researchers acknowledge that the issue is fraught with complexities. Receiving a formal diagnosis often helps people understand themselves better and tap greater support, but some adults already diagnosed say it comes with its own burdens, such as a stigmatising label and lower expectations for achievement. Whereby camouflaging often develops as a natural adaptation strategy to navigate reality. Autism was traditionally considered a male condition as more boys had a diagnosis than girls back in the 1990's but as science has evolved some psychologists have termed it the consequences of the extreme male brain - where the suggestions have been intimated that women mask the behaviours, and therefore have been historically under diagnosed which has further opened the floodgates.

Because so many more boys are diagnosed with Autism than girls are, clinicians don't always think of Autism when they see girls who are quiet or appear to be struggling socially. Often girls have been shuffled from one agency or doctor to another, often misdiagnosed with other conditions, not realising girls may need just as much support as boys do. In a few small studies starting in 2016, Researchers confirmed that, at least among women with high intelligence quotients (IQ), camouflaging is common. They also noted possible gender differences that help girls escape clinicians' notice: Whereas boys with autism might be overactive or appear to misbehave their behaviours were more noticeable than girl's behaviours.

To evaluate some of these methods, in the United Kingdom M Lai assistant professor of psychiatry at the University of Toronto in Canada surveyed 55 women, 30 men and 7 individuals who are either transgender or 'other' gendered, all diagnosed with Autism. They asked what motivates these individuals to mask their Autism traits and what techniques they use to achieve their goal. Some of the participants reported that they camouflage in order to connect with friends, find a good job or meet a romantic partner. Camouflaging well can land you a lucrative job. It can help you get through social interaction without there being a spotlight on your behaviour. Others said they camouflage to avoid punishment, to protect themselves from being shunned or attacked, or simply to be seen as 'normal.

Some people on the Spectrum believed if they had been diagnosed as a child, their parents might have understood them better. Some might have also avoided a long history of depression and self-harm. One of the main reasons some went down the route of a diagnosis was because they knew they were different but didn't know why and were bullied quite badly at school.

The vast majority of people diagnosed later in life say that not knowing early on that they have Autism hurt them. In a small 2016 study, Many described experiences of sexual abuse. They also said that, had their condition been known, they would have been less misunderstood and alienated at school. They might have also received much needed support sooner. When people discover and read up on the Autism Spectrum they often feel as having an "a ha" moment "this is me"! It can be a major turning point where everything starts to make sense.

It's only after a diagnosis that a person may ask, which parts of myself are an act and which parts of me have been hidden or what actually is the real me? Self identify, is key; then you can start to replay the past with this new insight. So for many people, this can happen late in life after years of camouflaging in a very uncontrolled, destructive and subconscious way, with many mental health problems as a consequence. Realising that you are not broken, that you simply have a different neurology from the majority of the population and that there is nothing wrong with you the way you are means that you will not hide who I am just to fit in or make other people more comfortable.

What about the people that never ever recognise they may have Autistic traits?

Yes this inevitably will happen and there will be people out there that will shun and suggest that the contents of this book are a load of garbage, and everybody is entitled to their opinion and that's their right. We would say that they have black and white dichotomous thinking. Others learn to make camouflaging work for them, mitigating its negative effects. They may use masking techniques when they first make a new connection, but over time become more authentically themselves. Many people out there won't like change, because they are used the behaviours and coping mechanisms they have employed for so long and others may be clearly offended by the fact that they may just exist somewhere on this spectrum indeed. We hope in sharing this we learn to take care of ourselves better the strategy is self-awareness. If not, suck it up and deal and it. It is a really difficult struggle, making loads of mistakes along the way with simply no choice. I can only say from my perspective as an undiagnosed Autistic had I been labelled maybe I wouldn't have tried so hard and achieved all the things I've achieved in life including writing this book!

I've have had depression does that mean I am on the Spectrum?

As yet no clinical studies have been taken on all these in society as a whole who have ever suffered with depression. However Spectrum News.org.uk opinion states that depression is more common among autistic people than it is among the general population, based on both clinical experience and research evidence. Some researchers argue that it is actually the most common mental health condition in Autistic people. It still isn't clear how common it actually is as reported rates of depression in Autism vary widely. There's growing evidence that depression is significantly underdiagnosed in this group.

Detecting depression is critical, the mood disorder can have devastating consequences on quality of life, and it increases the risk of suicidal thoughts and behaviours in Autistic adults. In 2018 Nearly half of adults with autism will experience clinical depression in their lifetime, according to research published in the Journal of Abnormal Child Psychology. On the one hand, it may be only natural to feel anxious and depressed when you think you may have Autism and that it deeply affects your daily life. On the other hand, it can seem like injustice piled on top of unfairness to have to deal with both ASD and severe depression or anxiety at the same time, but no clear link has yet been established scientifically because depression in autism is complicated and researchers are still understanding what matches fully to the spectrum.

What job do I do on the Spectrum?

Many people have many successful jobs based on what their strongest attributes are. If you are a good communicator and many people are you might have maintained a job dealing with the general public as sales person as you have the gift of the gab, you may not necessarily be on the social exclusion end of the spectrum scale as many earlier pioneers of the autistic spectrum once thought. Many Aspies have maintained and do maintain successful careers in their area of specialism, some Aspies are still finding themselves, and have had several careers across a wide variety of subjects and are still discovering what's best for them and their behaviour traits.

We would suggest that if you have a hobby specialism or interest and you feel most comfortable with it – go for it. Try and make this your career if you can, it's what you feel most comfortable that works for you. For years as a dyslexic myself I shied away from writing, and developed unhealthy coping mechanisms covering up my dyslexia from others, and as a visual creative I worked for many years in the TV & Film Industry making films using my visual and visionary capabilities. Now with the advent of modern computer software and an excellent editor I am able to write or rather type my words on a computer more proficiently. Today in my later years I now find the peace and harmony of writing more suitable to my temperament because it requires structure organisation and vision which I managed to harness in my early career days. Every one's different try to embrace it, as you get older on the spectrum your abilities and behaviours might change, or they may not. As I suggested in Chapter 11 a visual overview, you will have a flair in one or more of 7 areas which include Music, Sport, Language, Science, Business, Maths or Creativity. For myself they are Business and Creativity.

NB: For languages these will also include the English language where journalism may be a preferred career choice.

There are many many professions that fall into these areas. Always remember use your gift. The National Autistic Society believe people with autism have some very valuable skills which can be applied in the workplace. They might have very good attention to detail, or be really good at sticking to routines and timetables. Therefore, they are likely to be very punctual and reliable. Everyone has different skills but there will always be something. Employers are opening up the gateway now to help prospective employees experiencing difficulties in certain areas, and human resources managers are making varying adjustments in the workplace to help people on the spectrum feel more at ease. What these adjustments are depends on the individual's needs and requirements, which can include desk adjustment, adjusted lighting, noise-cancelling headphones, amended working hours, more opportunities to work from home, regular catch-up meetings with a manager, assistance with work planning, scheduled breaks including morning and afternoon, regular use of meeting rooms for working or adjusted hours. Outside of the office these can include, reduced travel to different work locations, and help with creating a work and travel routine. To some people these may seem insignificant things but to some people they can make a huge difference to their working day to avoid information overload and avoid meltdowns. As understanding grows about what our needs are in the work place, the more we feel relaxed.

Because autism is still widely misunderstood by most people, those diagnosed with the disorder can find it difficult to get a job or training for a career. The difficulty in finding jobs for people with autism, especially the more severe cases, can have a knock-on effect that impacts the rest of their lives. Having a healthy professional life is a crucial component of an overall balanced lifestyle and positive outlook.

Do all Aspie's have an affinity with Animals?

Recent research indicates autistic participants had a 70% success rate when identifying the emotional expressions of faces in Animals, and in contrast had only a 50% success rate in Humans. People with autism are often characterised as having difficulties with theory of mind abilities such as emotion recognition. However, rather than being a pervasive deficit of 'mindblindness,' a number of studies suggests these difficulties vary by context, and when people with autism mind read non-human agents, such as animals or cartoons these abilities improve. This study was by Liam Cross, Myles Farha and Gray Atherton Aug 2019.

I have a parent/grandparent that's an addict does that mean I will be one too?

It has been estimated that 40–60% of the vulnerability to developing an addiction is due to genetics. Addiction vulnerability is an individual's risk of developing an addiction during his or her lifetime. There are a range of genetic and environmental risk factors for developing an addiction that vary across the population. Genetic and environmental risk factors each account for roughly half of an individual's risk for developing an addiction so the contribution from epigenetic risk factors to the total risk is unknown. However if a grandparent had an addiction ie: alcohol a child or grandchild niece/nephew/uncle may develop another different addiction or the same one. Even in individuals with a relatively low genetic risk, exposure to sufficiently high doses of an addictive drug for a long period of time (e.g.weeks or months) can result in an addiction. In other words, anyone can become an addict under the right circumstances. Research is working toward establishing a comprehensive picture of the neurobiology of addiction vulnerability, including all factors at work in propensity for addiction.

Being on the Spectrum Can I live a happy life?

You are no different from the person you were yesterday, this book is not to say that those with autism cannot lead a happy fulfilling life, of course you can, but many people may need intense support and resources to achieve that and hopefully this book will help you to understand your thinking more and more and to understand the condition better.

Hopefully understanding the responsibility identifying the conditions when it's part of normal human variation is all part of life's richness, so whether you are peacemaker, challenger, enthusiast, loyalist, investigator, achiever, or a perfectionist, whether you hold resentments, flatter others, fantasise about the future, appear vain, stingy, display cowardness, plan excessively, love uncontrollably, be a truth seeker, have faith, wisdom, transparency, possess hope, display freedom of will. Whether life makes you corrupt, feel unloved, worthless, whether life makes you feel you have little or no identity or significance, feel helpless, incapable or incompetent, whether you feel un supported or lack guidance. Whether you are personally unfulfilled, trapped or deprived, harmed, controlled or violated, or feel loss fragmentation or separation. Whatever your life experiences have been, you have within yourself the ability to have a happy life with deeper understanding of your stress points and your instinctual self preservation energies.

Danielle Hampson Biography

Danielle Hampson has volunteered for the last 8 years as a Trustee for South Liverpool Domestic Abuse Services where she assists with the organisations PR & Marketing and has currently line managed and supervised the staff and volunteers. She retrained as a CBT Integrative counsellor psychotherapist in 2016 and obtained a BSC (Hons) Degree in Counselling and Psychotherapy from Stafford University. Danielle has worked concurrently both privately and in a voluntary capacity at Voice 4 Change in Waterloo Bootle Merseyside and dedicates her time working with victims and perpetrators of domestic violence, and a variety of mental health conditions including alcohol, drug abuse and substance misusers including a wide range of complex personality disorders. Danielle currently runs Anger Manager Programmes with perpetrator clients and has counselled well over a thousand hours per year to many victims in a voluntary capacity. Danielle is also a volunteer counsellor for the South Liverpool Trust working with ethnic minority women which includes Traveller, Jewish, Deaf and BAMER groups. She was a volunteer for Jewish Women's Aid in Merseyside and for the last 17 years has mentored families and friends of alcoholics and substance misusers through the charitable organisation Al Anon where she recently undertook the volunteer role of PI Co ordinator for the region covering Stafford, Sandbach, Hereford, Chester, North Wales, Merseyside, Wirral Southport, Wilmslow and South Manchester/Cheshire. Danielle was also a Volunteer Schools Education Advisor for the NSPCC and Childline School Service in 2016. Danielle is an active forum member of the Truth Project part of the IICSA and has a special interest in Autism and its links to Child Sexual Abuse, Domestic Violence and Substance Misuse. Prior to this she worked as both a TV Producer and an Entertainment Publicist and has worked extensively promoting a range of diverse clients and their projects within the field of Sport, Business, TV, Film & Music for more than 25 years. Over the years Danielle made documentaries and films about the personalities she has promoted and worked successfully as a TV Commercials Producer. As a former broadcaster for Radio City in Merseyside and BBC GMR in Manchester, Danielle sat on the board of Directors at alldayPA.com. In 2015 Danielle was voted 4th in the UK Jewish Chronicle Mench Awards (Good Person) & a runner up for Merseyside Woman Of The Year as Hidden Jewish Community Gem. She has two children aged thirteen and eleven with Special Needs Aspergers Syndrome and ADHD Danielle is a single mother. Am I on The Spectrum? Is Danielle's first self help publication.

Printed in Great Britain
by Amazon